UNDERSTANDING
Denise Levertov

Understanding Contemporary American Literature

Matthew J. Bruccoli, *Editor*

UNDERSTANDING
Denise
LEVERTOV

by HARRY MARTEN

UNIVERSITY OF SOUTH CAROLINA PRESS

for
Abraham and Ann

Copyright © University of South Carolina 1988

Published in Columbia, South Carolina, by the
University of South Carolina Press

Manufactured in the United States of America

LIBRARY OF CONGRESS
Library of Congress Cataloging-in-Publication Data

Marten, Harry.
  Understanding Denise Levertov / by Harry Marten.
    p. cm. — (Understanding contemporary American literature)
  Bibliography: p.
  Includes index.
  ISBN 0-87249-578-7. ISBN 0-87249-579-5 (pbk.)
  1. Levertov, Denise, 1923- —Criticism and interpretation.
I. Title. II. Series.
PS3562.E8876Z79 1988
811'.54—dc19   88-17617
                                                        CIP

CONTENTS

EDITOR'S PREFACE

Understanding Contemporary American Literature has been planned as a series of guides or companions for students as well as good nonacademic readers. The editor and publisher perceive a need for these volumes because much of the influential contemporary literature makes special demands. Uninitiated readers encounter difficulty in approaching works that depart from the traditional forms and techniques of prose and poetry. Literature relies on conventions, but the conventions keep evolving; new writers form their own conventions—which in time may become familiar. Put simply, *UCAL* provides instruction in how to read certain contemporary writers—identifying and explicating their material, themes, use of language, point of view, structures, symbolism, and responses to experience.

The word *understanding* in the series title was deliberately chosen. Many willing readers lack an adequate understanding of how contemporary literature works; that is, what the author is attempting to express and the means by which it is conveyed. Although the criticism and analysis in the series have been aimed at a level of general accessibility, these introductory volumes are meant to be applied in conjunction with the works they cover. Thus they do not provide a substitute for the works and authors they introduce, but rather prepare the reader for more profitable literary experiences.

M. J. B.

ACKNOWLEDGMENTS

Denise Levertov's poems and prose, and selections of poems by William Carlos Williams and by Rainer Maria Rilke, translated by J. B. Leishman, are reprinted by permission of New Directions. Portions of this study were originally published in *New England Review*, now *New England Review and Bread Loaf Quarterly*, and in *Sagetrieb*. I am grateful to the editors of these journals for permission to use material from my essays "Denise Levertov, *Life in the Forest*," *New England Review* 2 (1979): 162–64, and "Exploring the Human Community: The Poetry of Denise Levertov and Muriel Rukeyser," *Sagetrieb* 3 (Winter 1984): 51–61. My special thanks to Sydney Lea, editor of *New England Review and Bread Loaf Quarterly*, for his interest and support over the years. I am grateful to Denise Levertov for taking the time to talk with me in the summer of 1986, and for sharing with me a manuscript copy of *Breathing the Water*, and typescripts of her unpublished articles: "On the Need for New Terms," "Horses with Wings," "Gathered at the River: Background and Form." My work has been generously supported by a Humanities Faculty Development Grant from Union College. The staff of the Union College Library, particularly Reference Librarians Bruce

ACKNOWLEDGMENTS

Connolly and David Gerhan, helped in many ways. My thanks to colleagues Adrian Frazier, Jordan Smith, and Ruth Stevenson for sharing their insight, energy, and good conversation; to Kit Hathaway for his warmth and wisdom; to Martha Fleming for cheerfully helping to solve small biblical and medieval puzzles for me; to Peter Heinegg for similar help; and to William M. Murphy, always a model of what a scholar should aspire to, for his encouragement. I thank my colleague Jim McCord for two decades of friendship, during which I have never ceased to profit from his humor, openness, generosity, and intelligence, from his knowledge of contemporary literature and his ability to read with care and insight, from his encouragement and support. My greatest debts, as always, are to my parents, Abraham and Ann Marten, my sons Peter and Timothy, and, especially, to my wife, Ginit.

ABBREVIATIONS

References to Denise Levertov's books will be given parenthetically in the text when practical. I use the following titles and short titles (see Notes and Bibliography for full bibliographical information):

Books by Levertov

The Double Image (1946)	*Double Image*
Here and Now (1957)	*Here and Now*
Overland to the Islands (1958)	*Overland*
With Eyes at the Back of Our Heads (1959)	*Eyes*
The Jacob's Ladder (1961)	*Ladder*
O Taste and See (1964)	*Taste*
The Sorrow Dance (1967)	*Sorrow*
Relearning the Alphabet (1970)	*Relearning*
To Stay Alive (1971)	*Stay Alive*
Footprints (1972)	*Footprints*
The Poet in the World (1973)	*Poet*
The Freeing of the Dust (1975)	*Freeing*
Life in the Forest (1978)	*Life*
Collected Earlier Poems 1940–1960 (1979)	*Earlier Poems*
Light Up the Cave (1981)	*Light*
Candles in Babylon (1982)	*Candles*
Oblique Prayers (1984)	*Prayers*
Breathing the Water (1987)	*Breathing*

UNDERSTANDING
Denise Levertov

CHAPTER ONE

Understanding Denise Levertov: The Poet in Place

Career

Denise Levertov, claimed by both England and America as a poet of major importance, was born in 1923 in Ilford, Essex. Daughter of Paul Levertoff, a Russian Jew who became an Anglican priest, and Welshwoman Beatrice Spooner-Jones, Levertov has recently written that "My father's Hasidic ancestry, his being steeped in Jewish and Christian scholarship and mysticism, his fervor and eloquence as a preacher, were factors built into my cells. . . . Similarly, my mother's Welsh intensity and lyric feeling for Nature were not just the air I breathed but, surely, were in the body I breathed with."[1]

Educated at home save for formal ballet lessons, Levertov has called herself "a child of the London streets . . . a child of the Victoria and Albert Museum."[2] Learning from nature in expeditions to Wanstead and

Valentine parks, from reading literature at home, and from the art and history available in London's museums, Levertov quickly discovered her poetic vocation. She found, too, that "humanitarian politics came into my life early—seeing my father on a soapbox protesting Mussolini's invasion of Abyssinia; my father and sister both on soap-boxes protesting Britain's lack of support for Spain; my mother canvassing long before those events for the League of Nations Union."[3]

During World War II Levertov worked as a civilian nurse at St. Luke's Hospital, Fitzroy Square, London, writing at the time many of the poems that would be published by the Cresset Press in 1946 as *The Double Image*. A year later she married American writer Mitchell Goodman, moving with him to New York City at the end of 1948. There, in 1949, her son Nikolai was born. Though she published no new books, her poems were included in Kenneth Rexroth's anthology, *New British Poets*, in 1949, and new friendship with poet Robert Creeley resulted in the publication of her poems in Cid Corman's magazine *Origin* and in the *Black Mountain Review*.

Levertov has described the early 1950s as "transitional." Although she was back in Europe for a time in 1950–1951 while her husband, supported by the G.I. Bill, studied and wrote, she continued to establish her new home in New York. She did not produce many good poems but found the time for reading, talking,

CAREER

breathing "the air of American life" (*Poet* 67). In 1956, Levertov became an American citizen.

Eleven years after the appearance of her first book, Levertov published her first U.S. book, *Here and Now* (1957), and a year later her second, *Overland to the Islands* (1958). The two launched her as an American poet. In 1959, her first collection for James Laughlin's New Directions, *With Eyes at the Back of Our Heads*, appeared, establishing a publishing relationship that is still in place nearly thirty years later. Over the years, Levertov has written a dozen more volumes of poems, two collections of essays, and a volume of translations of Breton poet Guillevic. To date, her collected poems have been gathered in three volumes that cover the years 1940–60, 1960–67, and 1968–72. Widely acclaimed as one of America's most skilled, intelligent, and innovative poets, she is recognized, too, as an important activist-writer whose response in words and actions to "Life at War" (*Sorrow* 79) in Vietnam, Latin America, Detroit, and elsewhere, has helped stir the nation's conscience. Throughout her career, Levertov has stressed the interconnectedness of her writing, her commitment to social protest, and her work as a teacher at such diverse institutions as Drew University, City College of New York, Vassar College, University of California at Berkeley, MIT, Brandeis University, Tufts University, and Stanford University. She has not only written poems and prose protesting government policy at home and abroad, the Vietnam War, the nuclear arms race, and public indifference to environmental issues, but she has acted upon her convictions. In 1968, public protest and private life came together most dramatically, as her husband was indicted with Dr. Benjamin Spock for conspiring to oppose the military draft. In the decades since, Levertov has continued to participate energetically in rallies, marches, and human rights demonstrations. The force of her engagement with public concerns as well as private subjects resonates through her art and life.

Poetry editor of *The Nation* in 1961, and again from 1963–65, member of the American Academy and Institute of Arts and Letters, recipient of many awards, including a Guggenheim Foundation Fellowship in 1962, the Lenore Marshall Poetry Prize for the 1975 publication of *The Freeing of the Dust*, and the Elmer Holmes Bobst Award in 1983, Levertov currently divides her time between residence in Massachusetts and California, where she teaches at Stanford University part of each year. The recent publication of *Breathing the Water* (1987) confirms her reputation as one of America's major writers.

Overview

Much of the poetry written since the Second World War seems to have followed directions that lead at one extreme to what modern American poet Conrad Aiken called "jejune precisions of artifice and formalism, . . . snug enclosures of wit and irony,"[4] and at another to what the contemporary poet Louis Simpson labeled a "Revolution in Taste" in which "we are stuck with our sweating selves" while poetry becomes "almost exclusively a means of self-expression."[5] In the last decade, perhaps inevitably, a reaction to extremes of detachment and disclosure has set in, resulting in a poetry of discourse that according to critic and poet Robert Pinsky "is primarily neither ironic nor ecstatic."[6]

Amidst poetry that is often alienating in its brittle displays of wit, its extreme privacy, its use of rhetoric to avoid both self-absorption and irony, Denise Levertov's verse has stood fast and stood out. For four decades she has offered an alternative to systematically detached verse that seems to claim its authority strictly in the intricacies of its formal surfaces and to a predominantly self-centering verse that moves readers with its power of confession. Nor is her verse a product of what the critic Charles Altieri has called "civilized"[7] communication, claiming the authority of carefully executed rhetoric. Virtually from its beginnings, Levertov's has been an art of community, of relationships both inside and outside of the poem. Her verses are both impassioned and scrupulously controlled, neither simply exploring nor eschewing self, but uncovering and making known the relationship of self to the world. They find their authority in the ways feeling and form conjoin.

In her more than fifteen books of poems Levertov has proven herself a poet of changes, convinced that the writer's obligation is *"to take personal and active responsibility for his words"* (*Poet* 114), while recognizing that the poet's task is "to clarify . . . not answers but the existence and nature of questions" (45). Steadily, from her first mannered poems to the most recent spiritual meditations of *Breathing the Water,* she has offered a mix of communicative possibilities: the lyric together with the narrative, the visionary with the reportorial, the mythic with the everyday, intense intimacies and public proclamations. The reader who would know Levertov's work in all its variety of modes and moods must recognize that at its defining center mind and eye are linked. Such poetry reveals the process of thought and feeling rather than attending primarily to the product.

Looking outward and inward, Levertov presents poetic themes that clarify the nature of the artist as observer and imaginative creator. A crucial goal of her writing is to represent the world as it is. She describes the natural environment and displays the commonplace routines of human experience. At the same time, her verses are an effort to comprehend and represent the political disorders—from the Second World War to the Vietnam War and beyond—that threaten to overwhelm human potential. Levertov suggests that too many live with tunnel vision, their perception narrowed by ego or by materialistic ambitions, ignorant of their surroundings and their history. She seeks to increase her readers' awareness by reporting, meditating upon, and imaginatively transforming things-as-they-are.

OVERVIEW

Suggesting that in order to know the world one must know oneself, Levertov frequently centers her poems on explorations of her relationship to her ancestors, her parents, her sister, husband and son, her domestic responsibilities, and her role as a self-aware woman. As she expands her reach to include poems that are immediately concerned with matters of current affairs and public policy, or reaches further still, composing poems that take as their primary subject the relationship of man to a spiritual presence that is more than human though visible in nature, Levertov defines an important theme that amidst chaos there is an essential order linking all experience. It is the poet's role as witness, seer, and shaper, to discover and reveal the discord and the harmony. Levertov declares the interconnectedness of public and private knowing, of the consciousness and the unconscious, of observation and emotion, contemplation and participation.

In many ways a traditionalist in her concern for meticulous attention to craft, though a technical innovator, Levertov insists that poetic structure and content are inseparable. She does not typically organize her poems according to preestablished conventions of rhyme, meter, and stanzaic patterns that would allow the reader to perceive meanings within a set of received expectations. Rather, she often compels her readers to discover distinct and particular meanings in the process of working through unpredictable sonic and visual tensions. Thus, she is attentive to the way particular meanings are revealed by varying line-lengths, line-breaks, and line-placements. Words are seen surprisingly isolated against the white of the page or are perceived with abrupt stops followed by unexpected silences, or they run together and are heard as explosions of uninterrupted sound.

Furthermore, Levertov frequently manipulates sound patterns, clustering heavily alliterative language amidst noticeably spare or flat-sounding words. She mixes colloquial diction with formal diction, and direct speech with figurative language. Her poems often turn on the tensions established by a mixture of immediate, natural, sensory images, and more abstract and suggestive dreamlike images, or on the juxtapositions of images found in public documents, speeches, newspaper headlines, with those drawn from literature, myth, folklore and fairy tales, or personal experiences. For Levertov poetry is discovery, and her techniques of composition, seeking forms particular to each occasion, ensure that her readers will be drawn into the process of each reading experience anew, unable to fall back on preconceived expectations of poetic perception.

Describing the beginnings of her career, Levertov once observed that she "developed from a British Romantic with almost Victorian background."[8] The American poet Kenneth Rexroth, an early anthologizer of her work, linked her loosely with a diverse group of post–Second World War British neoromantic poets whose work exhibits a "ruminative melancholy" of the sort displayed in Stephen Spender's and J. B. Leishman's popular and influential translations of German poet

Rainer Maria Rilke (1875–1926). Noting that this sort of verse has "a dreamy, nostalgic sorrow about it, reminiscent of autumn evenings . . . lights on the river," Rexroth observed that "In poets like Denise Levertov this tendency reaches its height in slow, pulsating rhythms, romantic melancholy and undefined nostalgia. Once these qualities would have been considered blemishes, today they are outstanding virtues."[9]

But even the early, sometimes amorphous, evocative poems of *The Double Image* reveal glimpses of what was to be her lifelong effort to "accept and explore" all that a poet should incorporate: "the gift of the senses, the gifts of memory and language and intellectual discernment, and . . . the gift of intuition which transcends the limitations of deductive reasoning."[10] Though her early verses tend at times to be too heavily laden with sentiment or with metaphysical diction, they set out to examine the relationship of the individual to the world in dreamscapes, meditations, and observations. Defining a sense of place and beginning to explore the ways the poet's sensibility both shapes and is shaped by it, Levertov reveals the interconnections of self and others. Though not completely accomplished, her poems of love and loss, of crises and routines of life in war-torn Europe, reveal the possibilities of language for expressing relationships and contrasts.

Levertov's second book was published more than a decade later. By the time *Here and Now* was released in 1957 and its companion volume, *Overland to the Islands*, in 1958, she was living in the United States, and her work had already begun to show the influence of American voices and subjects. As she describes the changes and developments of those years:

Marrying an American and coming to live here [New York City] while still young was very stimulating to me as a writer for it necessitated the finding of new rhythms in which to write, in accordance with new rhythms of life and speech. My reading of William Carlos Williams and Wallace Stevens, which began in Paris in 1948; of Olson's essay, 'Projective Verse'; conversations and correspondence with Robert Duncan; a renewed interest through Buber in the Hasidic ideas with which I was dimly acquainted as a child . . . have all been influential.[11]

In the decade from the late 1940s through the 1950s, Levertov felt "the stylistic influence of William Carlos Williams" as "a very necessary and healthful one, without which I could not have developed . . . [into] an American poet of any vitality."[12] Williams (1883–1963), a physician and distinguished poet from New Jersey, perhaps more successfully than any writer of the century sought to discover and define a uniquely American poetic idiom and rhythm. His conviction that the poet must pay direct attention to the world before him, precisely using his eye, ear, and shaping imagination to achieve an authentic perception of his immediate experience, strongly influenced the post-1945 generation of American poets.

OVERVIEW

Williams's effort to provide for himself and others "a context of objective, anti-metaphysical aesthetic intent in order to free poetry from the entanglement of . . . sentimental intellectualism"[13] was salutary for Levertov, helping her attend better to the importance of exact representation of her environment while she tightened her images and lines. But Williams's influence was most profoundly felt in Levertov's sympathy for the workings of his imagination, his conviction of the interconnectedness of the ordinary with the sensuous and intuitive. His ideas and work resonate in Levertov's definition of the imagination as "the power of perceiving analogies and of extending this power from the observed to the surmised. . . . Rather than breathing life into the dust . . . I see it as perceiving the life inherent in the dust."[14]

As the title suggests, the poems of *Here and Now* concentrate upon the immediate experience of "things as they are" as the poet observes her new American environment. Levertov is attentive to the play of color and light on particular scenes at precise moments, and she records carefully both the shapes of distinct objects and the impressions of visual forms seen in relation to one another for contrast or coherence. She writes of space and of the people who inhabit it and discovers in the process that things are rarely only what they appear to be, even to a careful observer of the physical. Describing local histories, recounting the activities and speech of ordinary people, recreating scenes from her own experiences, Levertov recognizes that facts spring to life as they are surprised, delineated, and transformed by the shaping imagination. Using myth and metaphor to enrich images and manipulating line- and word-rhythms to create tensions and relieve them, Levertov not only observes, but envisions the creative relationship of man and his surroundings.

Taking her readers on a magical voyage *Overland to the Islands* in her third book, Levertov more emphatically adds a dimension of fairy tale and myth to her poetic explorations. While she continues to take the measure of what her eye sees and what her hearing and touch perceive, she seems increasingly to attend to the way the worlds of eye and mind define each other. In poems that explore family memories and examine family histories, describe sights on the streets in New York and Mexico, and meditate upon personal relationships, she claims for her subject the mysterious workings of the imagination on experience.

Writing about her "Illustrious Ancestors" (*Earlier Poems* 77), a distinguished Hasidic rabbi and a Welsh tailor-teacher-preacher, Levertov uncovers her link to a creative line which both explains and confirms her own developing creative tendencies. For as she partly perceives and partly creates them, both men embody a creative lesson suggesting the necessity of close attention to the world before one, and acknowledging too that human experience is fraught with mystery. Sensitive to the mystery and convinced of the importance of direct communication, Levertov writes poems that explore domestic spaces and imagined territories, revealing the co-existence of the commonplace and the remarkable.

With Eyes at the Back of Our Heads (1959) seems both to sum up and expand the goals and achievements of Levertov's first decade and a half of growth as a writer. Always clarifying what can be done when the eye records, the intellect interprets, and the imagination transfigures the world, the book offers a portrait of what the poet, transcribing a Toltec Indian poem, has called "*The true artist: capable, practicing, skillful,*" who "*maintains dialogue with his heart, meets things with his mind*" and "*composes his objects, works dexterously, invents; / arranges materials . . . makes them adjust*" ("The Artist," *Eyes* 4). This is a book of changes and renewals, delineating the reciprocal nature of man's relationship with the natural world and with his created environment. With poems that range from didactic parable to recreated folk and fairy tales, contemporary myths and meditations to observations of the occurrences and recurrences that mark relationships and day to day activities, Levertov places her readers at the center of an effort to know the world in all its variety.

In the decade of the 1960s, Levertov's work grew more assured and inventive technically and reached farther thematically. *The Jacob's Ladder* (1961), *O Taste and See* (1964), and *The Sorrow Dance* (1966), collect a variety of short lyrics and poetic sequences, nonmetrical but rhythmically and melodically complex experiments in what Levertov recently called "Exploratory form." As she writes, taking her terms from nineteenth-century English poet Gerard Manley Hopkins, "the options for [the] articulation" of the "inscape of the subject," or its essential form, and "the instress of its perception"—or its form revealed in the energy of its design and meaning—"are *explored* . . . in ways which result in a form peculiar to that occasion."[15] Her poems in this period of unusual creative activity are both more explicitly sexual and more emphatically social than any she had attempted earlier. Whether she is describing the condition of women in "Hypocrite Women" (*Taste* 70), depicting "The Ache of Marriage" (5), exploring the human potential for evil in "During the Eichmann Trial" (*Ladder* 61), or just beginning to recognize and explain the terrible consequences of "Life at War" (*Sorrow* 79) in Vietnam, Levertov seeks to counter socially imposed or self-constructed censorships.

Seeking to awaken her readers to social responsibilities, and simultaneously to have them recognize that outer vision requires inner knowledge, Levertov turns increasingly for her subjects to history, headlines, and intensely personal memories and experiences. Readers discover in her poems the conviction that the private and public life resonate within one another, each clarifying, defining, challenging, and enriching the other. Her poetic world is a fluid one where interiors and exteriors are best perceived as concurrent.

Matching form to feeling, experimenting with syntax, line-break, line length, image, and sound, Levertov seeks a variety of poetic possibilities to make her readers aware of all that is alive "to the imagination's tongue." They are to recognize in themselves and in the world "grief, mercy, language," and they are, in the poet's poems and with her help, to "breathe them, bite, / savor, chew, swallow, transform" them ("O Taste and See," *Taste* 53).

By the late 1960s, with the United States enmeshed in a seemingly ceaseless war, Levertov, like many of her contemporaries, found herself writing more public poetry of outrage and lamentation. She explained that her goal was to blend the personal and the public so that her poems would not be categorizable. Although Levertov did not always manage to spin the didactic and lyrical into a seamless whole, the best poems of *Relearning the Alphabet* (1970), *To Stay Alive* (1971), *Footprints* (1972), and *The Freeing of the Dust* (1975) offer powerful social observations and commentary without reducing experience to shrill propaganda. In a great variety of forms, ranging from brief elegies to experimental narratives that mix found art with imagined, Levertov protests war, seeking, not simply to inform her readers, but to move them to understanding and action.

As the title of her 1970 volume suggests, she was relearning the alphabet, finding new forms for expression so as not to lose her voice in the anguish and horror of the time. *To Stay Alive*, published the following year, "a record of one person's inner/outer experience of America during the 60's and the beginning of the 70's" (ix), was in large part a reshaping into a new configuration of poems written earlier. The very act of seeking to make new forms from old, generating fresh creative energies from materials that directly communicate the terrors of the war years, suggests an affirmation of human potential that faces without denial the truths of limit as well as promise. In the bleakest times of turmoil and unrest in 1968 and 1969, when it often seemed to the poet that the only choice might be "Revolution or death" ("Notebook," *Relearning* 92),[16] Levertov's poems cast a light into the dark. Revealing the violence and chaos of that troubled time, she nonetheless affirmed in her poems of caring and commitment a spirit of community and a promise of possibility that could outlast hate.

But not all the poems of this period are political. *Footprints* is essentially a collection of brief lyric meditations on domestic and aesthetic topics, and all four books offer "illumination[s] of dailiness" ("Brass Tacks," *Footprints* 40). *The Freeing of the Dust* in particular matches its explorations of public issues with an important grouping of poems that explore private events. In a surprising reflection of the world at war, Levertov writes of a collapsing marriage, discovering in pain and sorrow a similar promise of renewal in the recognition of human energy and caring.

Levertov's friend, American poet Muriel Rukeyser, once declared that during times when the human spirit is in crisis we become aware of "our need for each other and . . . for ourselves. We call up our fullness; we turn and act. We begin to be aware of correspondences."[17] Whether Levertov was essentially looking outward in these years to face the world or inward to discover the deep well of self and private relationships, she continued to confirm "correspondences," exploring the crucial role of the creating imagination in bridging even seemingly disparate experiences. As the long poem, "Conversation in Moscow," from *The Freeing of the Dust* suggests, one must maintain dialogue between individual perceptions and the community's, as well as between professions and cultures.

In the last ten years, while continuing to decipher daily experience, to reveal and examine the "foul / dollops of History / each day thrusts at us" (*Prayers* 35) from Latin America, Asia, the Middle East, and to explore the workings of the creative imagination, Levertov seems to have become increasingly convinced that the exercise of the imagination moves one toward faith. Her most recent works have evolved toward a vision of the mysteries of human experience that confirms religious conviction. *Life in the Forest*, published in 1978, seems both a stocktaking and a threshold book for Levertov, affirming artistic continuities and offering new directions. At the heart of the collection are a series of poems that describe the death of the poet's mother. Explaining with sadness and anger the pain and indignity of the old woman's dying, Levertov still affirms in the process the worth and dignity of her life. Taking a hard look at the harsh realities of aging, the poet reveals, nonetheless, a vision of energy that outlasts the body; what was achieved remains vivid in memory and in example for those left behind. Levertov confirms, albeit only after a struggle and still with serious doubts and anxieties, some sense of design even in the face of the worst vision of life's ending.

Reflecting writers as diverse as Italian poet and novelist Cesare Pavese (1908–50), and Russian physician, playwright, short story writer Anton Chekhov (1860–1904), *Life in the Forest* reminds its readers that the past is luminous in the present. The spirit of coherence amidst change that emerges in this collection, marked by Pavese's gritty objectivity and Chekhov's delicate and exact realism, bursts forth in Levertov's books of the 1980s: *Candles in Babylon* (1982), *Oblique Prayers* (1984), and *Breathing the Water* (1987). Here, in what seems in retrospect a kind of logical extension of her exploration of the mystery of experience, Levertov moves toward a position of Christian belief. In a recent essay she observes that "the imagination . . . is the perceptive organ through which it is possible . . . to experience God.[18]

Not all the poems of these volumes make the subject of belief central. But even those that explicitly examine such subjects as family, politics, art, and aesthetics often seem charged with energies springing from a perception of forces beyond the individual that are part of the shape of experience. In *Candles in Babylon*, Levertov's new poetry of belief for an "Age of Terror" (*Candles* 71) is most vividly realized in the long "Mass for the Day of St. Thomas Didymus" (108). Here the poet declares the importance of faith that will not deny doubt. *Oblique Prayers* offers revelations of spiritual conviction

OVERVIEW

in vivid translations of contemporary French poet Jean Joubert's natural landscapes and mindscapes and in a variety of poems "Of God and of the Gods" (*Prayers* 69) that suggest a complex harmony of all created things. Most recently, *Breathing the Water* even more confidently celebrates man's creative relationship to nature, affirming a palpable connection between the physical and the spiritual. Here, as throughout her career, Levertov's work reveals the impact of the great early twentieth-century German poet Rilke, whose poems in volumes such as *The Book of Hours* (1905) are important to her for their elegant beauty and because they so clearly embody Rilke's stated convictions that poems are not simply feelings but experiences and that the pursuit of art is an almost religious activity. Presenting variations on poems and themes by Rilke, creative conversations with the works of medieval visionaries Caedmon and Lady Julian of Norwich, observations on religious painting, architecture, and writing, Levertov suggests in *Breathing the Water* that divine revelation is clarified by, and clarifies, ordinary lives.

German Expressionist painter Oskar Kokoschka once stated that "there will be no portrait left of modern man because he has lost his face and is turning towards the jungle."[19] Few have put back the lines as clearly and vividly as Denise Levertov.

Notes

1. Denise Levertov, "Denise Levertov Writes," *The Bloodaxe Book of Contemporary Women Poets: Eleven British Writers*, ed. Jeni Couzyn (Newcastle-upon-Tyne: Bloodaxe, 1985) 75.

2. Kenneth John Atchity, "An Interview with Denise Levertov," *San Francisco Review of Books* March 1979: 6.

3. Levertov, "Denise Levertov Writes" 78.

4. Conrad Aiken, *Collected Criticism* (London: Oxford University Press, 1968) 101.

5. Louis Simpson, *A Revolution in Taste* (New York: Macmillan, 1978) 169.

6. Robert Pinsky, *The Situation of Poetry* (Princeton: Princeton University Press, 1976) 134.

7. Charles Altieri, "From Experience to Discourse: American Poetry and Poetics in the Seventies," *Contemporary Literature* 21 (1980): 193.

8. Denise Levertov, "Denise Levertov," *The New American Poetry: 1945–1960*, ed. Donald M. Allen (New York: Grove 1960) 441.

9. Kenneth Rexroth, ed., introd., *The New British Poets: An Anthology* (New York: New Directions, 1949) xvi, xxix–xxx.

10. Denise Levertov, "Horses With Wings," typescript of an unpublished article 13.

11. Levertov, "Denise Levertov" 441.

12. Levertov, "Denise Levertov" 441.

13. Denise Levertov, "The Ideas in the Things," *Ezra Pound and William Carlos Williams: The University of Pennsylvania Conference Papers*, ed. Daniel Hoffman (Philadelphia: University of Pennsylvania Press, 1983) 131.

14. Ian Reid, " 'Everyman's Land': Ian Reid Interviews Denise Levertov," *Southern Review* (Adelaide, Australia) 5 (1972): 233.

15. Denise Levertov, "On the Need for New Terms," typescript of an unpublished article 4.

16. The full title of the poem is "From a Notebook: October '68–May '69." My parenthetical citations of this poem are abbreviated to "Notebook" for the sake of concision.

OVERVIEW

17. Muriel Rukeyser, *The Life of Poetry* (New York: William Morrow, 1974) 169.

18. Denise Levertov, "A Poet's View," *Religion and Intellectual Life* 1 (Summer 1984): 53.

19. Oskar Kokoschka, quoted in Stanley Kunitz, *A Kind of Order, A Kind of Folly: Essays and Conversations* (Boston: Little, Brown, 1975) 129.

CHAPTER TWO

Beginnings: Poems
1940–1960

Some years after the publication of her first book, *The Double Image* (1946), Denise Levertov was called by Kenneth Rexroth "the baby of the New [English] Romanticism."[1] The implication, in the heyday of Welsh poet Dylan Thomas's highly mannered, intensely self-absorbed surrealism, was that the young poet was next in a line of visionary singers whose extravagant emotional music rejected the balance, wit, and intellection of poets in the "classic" mode such as W. H. Auden and C. Day Lewis.

By the time of her next two books, *Here and Now* (1957) and *Overland to the Islands* (1958), Levertov, having in the interim moved to the United States and grappled with the American idiom, came to be identified with a part of the American avant-garde which in attitudes toward form, language, and content, seemed to emphasize the substance of daily life rather than vision. She was often linked with poets like Robert Creeley and

BEGINNINGS

Robert Duncan, who were associated with Charles Olson at the experimental Black Mountain College in North Carolina and who were grouped around Olson's grab bag theory of "Projective Verse" with its emphasis on possibilities of new forms—what Olson called "COMPOSITION BY FIELD, as opposed to inherited line, stanza." In this view the poem was an open rather than a closed construction, an assemblage of words and ideas on the page, taking its shape from its content and from the rapid pace of its perceptions, rather than conforming to already established, and hence closed, formal structures. This was verse with new ideas of rhythm as well. As Olson declared, "the line comes (I swear it) from the breath, from the breathing of the man who writes, at the moment that he writes,"[2] rather than from a rigid notion of poetic metrics.

Barely hidden behind Olson's "Projectivism" lie other "isms." Ezra Pound's "Imagism" and "Vorticism" stressed movement and the energy of juxtaposed images: "The 'new form' . . . is not a mimicry of external life. It is energy cut into stone."[3] And the "Objectivism" of William Carlos Williams and of his friends George Oppen and Charles Reznikoff paid keen attention to the objects a poet writes of and to the distinct form of each poem. As Williams explained, "The poem, like every other form of art, is an object, an object that in itself formally presents its case and its meaning by the very form it assumes. . . . It must be the purpose of the poet to make of his words a new form: to invent, that is, an object consonant with his day."[4]

These movements marked Levertov's writing because the work of the individuals who defined them was important to her. Yet despite shifting critical tags and some obvious changes in both her poetic goals and methods, the British Romantic had not in a dozen years simply metamorphosed into a pragmatic American. Obviously nurtured by modern masters—Rilke, Pound, H. D. (Hilda Doolittle), and Williams foremost among them—and sharing poetic affinities with friends like Creeley and Duncan, whose creative trajectory seemed sometimes to intersect her own, Levertov followed her own lines of force from the first, refusing category in all things. "I cannot simply enter a ready-made structure; I have to find components and construct my own."[5]

At the heart of Levertov's work lies the "acknowledgement, and celebration, of mystery [which is] probably . . . the most consistent theme of my poetry from its very beginnings."[6] The "American" Levertov, rather than sloughing off her youngest poetic self, sought to unite the "spirit of here-and-now I had learned from Williams . . . with the romantic spirit of quest, of longing to wander toward other worlds" (*Poet* 80), seeking to bring together "for myself my sense of the pilgrim way with my new, American, objectivist-influenced, pragmatic, and sensuous longing for . . . a living-in-the-present" (69).

"Though I own a house and have steady work," Levertov wrote not long ago, "I am by nature, heritage, and as an artist, forever a stranger and pilgrim."[7] Yet, as she acknowledges, in essential ways she had never been sharply dislocated from a clearly defined and de-fining world of places inhabited in fact, in the imagina-tion, in memory. "I feel I am more like an airplant . . . one of those things—it doesn't suck blood out of what-ever it lives on, but it doesn't actually have roots—that doesn't really describe my feelings either, because I do feel that I have deep roots in the culture and experi-ences that I obtained as a child."[8]

Sensitive to being partly an outsider and so seeking a place to come to, yet powerfully attuned to the physi-cal and emotional resonances of the sensory and imagi-native worlds she inhabited, Levertov made the exploration of the relation of physical to imaginative places a thematic hallmark of her verse. Placements and displacements fill the poems of her sometimes elusive highly figured British period, and of her increasingly direct American moments, given shape in two sus-tained concurrent directions that her verse takes. "When I look back I see that there are certain recurrent themes. I feel two strains in two directions going on in my poetry currently. One is a development of a fairly tight . . . lyric poem that derives much of its imagery from somewhere close to the unconscious, a kind of dream level of image. And the other is a longer lined, more discursive poem, with a fictive or narrative ele-ment."[9] And always at the center is the effort to compre-hend the power of the imagination. As Levertov has observed, "The poet sees, and reveals in language, what is present but hidden—what Goethe . . . called the *open secret*."[10]

The early poems of the 1940s and early 1950s published in *The Double Image,* or gathered recently in *Collected Earlier Poems 1940–1960,* are acknowledged by the poet to have a certain "muzzy adolescent vagueness." Often the language is laced with abstract rhetorical flourishes that the drama and theme do not call for. Too, the lyric and narrative frames of reference carry the reader, sometimes nervously and inexplicably, from dreamlike flashes where the psyche rumbles in forests of fear and isolation, to myth-laden plots where nature is transformed, the human figure fractured, inanimate objects animated. Yet here Levertov lays down the themes of human relationships explored and of perceptual possibilities revealed and examined, which she will follow through a lifetime of writing. "During my early years in America I was rather embarrassed by my first, English book; but later I came to accept it . . . as showing intuitive signs . . . of qualities that link it with what I tried to do as I grew more aware of craft and what must underlie it. . . . the field has grown larger as I walked through it, one might say, but yes, it is the same field."[11]

"Listening to Distant Guns," Levertov's first published poem, ushers the reader with rhymes and regular meter into an unsettling world of contraries where the calm natural surface of things seems to deny, yet strangely reveals, the fearsome nature of war to the seeing and imagining eye and ear. The regularity of the lyric, almost sing-songish in its gathered iambics, its assonance and consonance, is all the more disturbing in its impassive, steady revelation of the destructive force that makes "roses tremble," and rooks in flight appear to be "battalions" that "dwindle near the hill." Here, where no sound breaks the hush of "evening's silent dream," and the "bloodless clarity of evening's sky / Betrays no whisper of the battle-scream" (*Earlier Poems* 3), the intruding human presence, a silent observer, reads into the scene what she *knows* to be true about the destructive moment taking place off in the distance. She confirms not only man's capacity for violence, but, simultaneously, the discomforting indifference on the face of things and the knowledge that any action, any recognition, cannot fail to affect the ways in which individuals comprehend and define the world. Levertov has begun here to announce a major theme—the interrelationship of personal and public perception. She tells us, as her friend Muriel Rukeyser once wrote, that poetry "is an art . . . expressing and evoking the moving relation between the individual consciousness and the world."[12]

The eight poems of *The Double Image* that are reprinted in Levertov's *Collected Earlier Poems* offer glimpses of a young writer feeling her way toward technical security. Some, like the highly stylized address "To Death"—"Enter with riches, enviable prince"—seem essentially derivative, presenting not experience so much as elaborate discourse with a distinctly metaphysical clang. "Your eager bride, the flickering moth that burns / upon your mouth, brings to your dark reserve / a glittering dowry of desire and dreams" (*Earlier*

Poems 24). Even a more personal and engaged poem, such as "The Barricade," substitutes manner for matter, elaborate literary conceit for direct observation or original imagining, telling a lost lover and the reader that "duplicity . . . gnaws the roots of love" or that

> . . . beyond the walls of dream,
> rising, unbroken battlements, to a sky
> heavy with constellations of desire,
> . . . barricades are grown
> too tall to scale . . . (22).

But there are others in *The Double Image* which, while still trying on styles, voices, and language, probe deeper, achieve more. "Durgan," another poem of lost love and missed connections, is wrapped in echoes of the early T. S. Eliot of "The Love Song of J. Alfred Prufrock" and "Rhapsody on a Windy Night," revealed in the fragmented human form that inhabits an insubstantial world: "enigmatic eyes" that "peer into mirrors"—"blind eyelids lifting to a coloured world," to experience the "waking dream of day." But the poem mingles such self-consciously high-toned and well-worn modernism with undisguised convincing statements of loss and separation. "But separate, apart, you are alive: / you have not died, therefore I am alone." Levertov mixes dark dreamlike visions of an absent lover, now become a "living ghost / . . . shade of a shade," with transforming but direct descriptive images of place that center the poem not only in the mind's eye, but in the speaker's solitary but not solipsistic present, where

BEGINNINGS

> Like birds, cottages white and grey
> alert on rocks are gathered, or low
> under branches, dark but not desolate;
> shells move over sand, or seaweed gleams
> with their clear yellow, as tides recede.
>
> (Earlier Poems 21)

The specific details of scene, the pattern, movement, and variations of color so immediately felt, an-
chor the poem. Reflecting the speaker's state of mind,
but not simply defined by it, the natural world so carefully observed even in the midst of psychic turmoil
helps to make real the impact of solitude by preventing
the poem from slipping away into a shadowy stylized
portrait of emotional angst. The speaker may feel, for
the moment, alone in the world, but the reader recognizes that she *is* in it, after all, and it was there before
her as it will be there after her. In this the reader grasps
the full feeling of solitude, of human smallness; here
too is the realization of continuity that holds desolation
at bay.

If "Durgan," fixing upon a private experience, begins to make known the interactions of interior and exterior perspectives, "Christmas 1944" is more public in
its view, expanding to take in the world of war and current affairs. This poem also echoes Eliot, announcing
the bleak wasteland modern man inhabits and envisions, where, with "fear knocking on the doors," "all
that stand[s] between us and the wind" are "A painted
bird . . . above the fire" and "a candle in the dark"
(*Earlier Poems* 25). However, it is not a personal night-

mare which in this season intrudes on the "Spindrift
sparkle and candles on the tree" that "make brave pre-
tence of light" (24). Rather, it is the realization of the
"shadow / over the atlas" cast by the ceaseless slaughter
of fighting in Europe. Yet the power of this broad
glimpse of one of history's "long sagas of sorrow" (25)
resides precisely in the rendering of an exactly detailed
picture of an individual's ordinary place—

> Bright cards above the fire . . .
> . . . .
> Evening already surrounds the curtained house,
> draws near, watches;
> gardens are blue with frost . . . (24).

—combined with and contrasting visions of human mis-
ery where "venom trickles from the open mouth of
death, / and trees are white with rage of alien battles"
(25). One must neither lose sight of, nor simply receive,
perceptions from the commonplace world. A sense of
place is defined by the inevitable intertwining of physical objects, personal emotion, and public responsibility,
however much that shakes the longing for comfortable
complacencies:

> Though we are safe
> in a flickering circle of winter festival
> we dare not laugh; or if we laugh, we lie,
> hearing hatred crackle in the coal,
> the voice of treason, the voice of love (25).

"Bravely in a land of dust," Levertov has "set out, as
pilgrims must" ("Ballad" 25) to explore the range of hu-

man possibility and limit, with her senses, her transforming imagination, her conscience.

"Writing poetry is a process of discovery" Levertov
said in a 1968 lecture at the University of Michigan.
"Not an isolation of intellectual awareness but an
awareness involving the whole self, a *knowing* . . . a
'being in touch,' " it reveals "the music of correspondences" (*Poet* 54). And the eleven years between the
publication of her first and second books were years of
crucial discoveries. As she has described the beginnings: "In the early spring of 1948 I was living in Flor-
ence, a bride of a few months, having married
American literature, it seemed, as well as an American
husband. Both of us haunted the U.S.I.S. library on the
via Tornabuoni . . . I to discover . . . the poetry of what
was to be my adopted country" (*Light* 196).

The work of William Carlos Williams was particularly exciting for her. "Though I knew with mysterious
certainty that his work would become an essential part
of my life, I had not yet heard enough American speech
to be able to hear his rhythms properly; his poems were
a part of the future, recognized but held in reserve"
(*Light* 196). Later Levertov could say that "Williams
showed me the way, made me listen, made me begin to
appreciate the vivid and figurative language sometimes
heard from ordinary present-day people, and the fact
that even when vocabulary was impoverished there was
some energy to be found in the here and now" (201).
With theories, by example, in friendship, Williams
helped the young writer who was "seeking . . . to en-

gage [her] capacities as a poet with the crude substance of dailiness" (*Poet* 67). Levertov's Williams was not "essentially prosaic, a putter-together of scraps of reportage merely" (264), but was one who "gave [her] instance after instance of how one's most ordinary experience could be shown in the poem as it was, invested with wonder."[13]

What Levertov has described as "Williams' interest in the ordinary, in the present, in local history as microcosm, in the lives and speech of ordinary people; and his unsentimental compassion, which illumined the marvellous in the apparently banal," is in evidence everywhere in *Here and Now* and *Overland to the Islands*.[14] It balances, enriches, tempers, but never contradicts, the pilgrim's vision-charged seeking after experience.

The poems of these two books, Levertov has come to realize, "should really have been in a single book together because of their interrelationships." They were "arbitrarily divided" when poet Weldon Kees (and San Francisco poet Lawrence Ferlinghetti after Kees' death), and then publisher and poet Jonathan Williams, requested collections at almost the same time. "Because the Kees/Ferlinghetti offer had come first, I offered Ferlinghetti first choice of all the poems I had by then accumulated . . . and gave Jonathan the 'rejects' plus what still newer work I had done in the intervening months" (*Earlier Poems* ix). Thus the opening poems of each volume clarify the goals and methods of both, whether offering a glimpse with the eye and mind's eye into "The Gypsy's Window" (*Here and Now*), or observ-

BEGINNINGS

ing and meditating on the "intently haphazard" (*Earlier Poems* 55) dancing steps of an ordinary dog whose example might carry the reader on an unlikely magic journey "Overland to the Islands."

Although very much a poem of persons ("an old / bandanna'd brutal dignified / woman"), place (New York City's Hudson St.), objects ("trivial plates," "the rosaries," "a narrownecked dark vase"), and simple action ("Watching the trucks go by, from stiff chairs / behind the window"), "The Gypsy's Window" invites the reader not into a world of facts but onto a "stage" where the operative word is "seems" not "is." Here transformations of the ordinary precede or occur simultaneously with simple perceptions, making the reader aware simultaneously of the thing before him and the ways the seeing eye and the human imagination alter them even in the act of seeing. The window first observed from the street "seems a stage / backed by imaginations of velvet, / cotton, satin, loops and stripes" (*Earlier Poems* 29). The reader realizes that the title of the poem suggests not only a space that looks out on (or is looked into from) the street, but a kind of magical glass through which one sees shapes changed or changing, fictions created and enacted, factual realities adjusted.

Direct descriptions of the scene accumulate in such a way as to create connotative as much as denotative meanings. Seemingly simple observations are juxtaposed with others, equally forthright. But in combination the images generate unusual and suggestive impressions. The "dark" of a "narrownecked" vase seems concentrated by placement against the bright pastel of "unopened yellow and pink / paper roses," just as the pastel color seems hardened against the generalized "dark" which in this moment is neither blue, nor black, nor any other concretely identified color. The contrast is vaguely disconcerting, as is the combination of the pictorially precise and constricted "narrownecked" with the amorphous "dark" which seems to dissolve into the undefined background space. While the poet notices a relaxed "lovely unconcern" about the mild chaos of "scattered" "trivial plates" which she can see from her vantage, the accumulating sense of restriction gathering in descriptions like that of the "narrownecked dark vase," the "unopened . . . / paper roses," the "stiff chairs / behind the window" creates a sense of tension in the scene. The juxtaposed open image ("a luxury of open red / paper roses" [*Earlier Poems* 29]), which the observer notices and sets amidst the rest, serves only to accent the disconcerting feeling of closure, of disquiet. And even the roses are somehow not quite right, being artificial, paper instead of petal.

Having seen and imaginatively transformed a scene, the chance observer arranges its human presences as if at the center of a complex drama taking place just beyond reach. There is not enough information to comprehend precisely what it is that moves within these two frozen figures, but both the mystery and the meaning seem to lie in the descriptions of "things" the speaker has already intuited and conveyed. Though the figures are simply "Watching the trucks go by" at the window, the reader feels the depth of passion that defines the lives of the two women who emerge from the unsettling background of closure and limit: "an old / bandanna'd brutal dignified / woman, a young beautiful woman / her mouth a huge contemptuous rose" (*Earlier Poems* 29).

As provocative as the transformed scene and hinted drama are, however, they are not, after all, what the poem focuses upon. Levertov has not only shown the reader a set of "things," and involved him in narrative speculations, but has demonstrated the process of imaginative creation, offering a recognition of the ways art and artifice mingle with the "real." "The courage / of natural rhetoric tosses to dusty / Hudson St. the chance of poetry, a chance / poetry gives passion to the roses." The reader recognizes with the poet that "the roses in the gypsy's window," seen after all to be in "a blue / vase" and not the imaginatively transforming "dark" one rendered by first impressions, "look real" though paper. But they seem real only in that they are "as unreal / as real roses" (*Earlier Poems* 29). The message, of course, is an old one: art and life are reciprocal, each taking shape and energy from the other. "The Gypsy's Window," at once a close observation, and an imagining, is also a meditation on the nature of creativity. Levertov demonstrates that poetry scorns neither thought nor thing. "The imagination," as she has explained writing of Williams, "does not reject its own sensory origins but illuminates them, and connects them with intellectual and intuitive experience."[15]

UNDERSTANDING DENISE LEVERTOV

Levertov further clarifies her goals and procedures in the title poem of her second volume. "Let's go," she begins in "Overland to the Islands," taking her direction, as if casually, from close attention to her immediate environment, "much as that dog goes, / intently haphazard" (*Earlier Poems* 55). The recommendation, allowing form to take its shape from discovery rather than from the imposition of a preconceived pattern, sounds a note that defines Levertov's themes and method throughout her career. If individuals want to manage creative journeys that are likely to strike the more reasonable or cautious among them as virtually impossible—over land to an island—they need not make outrageous or fantastic leaps. But they must trust their senses, their intuitive movements, their capacity for attentiveness to that which is before them, and their commitment to it and delight in it.

> Under his feet
> rocks and mud, his imagination, sniffing,
> engaged in its perceptions—dancing
> edgeways, there's nothing
> the dog disdains on his way,
> nevertheless he
> keeps moving, changing
> pace and approach but
> not direction . . . (55).

The poem ends quoting Rilke, enriching the immediate by putting readers in touch with the resonance of a literary inheritance. Those who are intent on their pur-

BEGINNINGS

poses, yet responsive to changes demanded by fresh perceptions, discover not only the way to an end, but in "'every step an arrival.' "

While the poem's statement is unconfusing and direct, more a forthright "telling" than a metaphoric "showing," Levertov's creative use of irregular rhythmic pause and line-break energizes imagery to engage the reader fully in the experience of discovery. Surrounding short lines (2,3,5,8, and 9, e.g.) with long ones above and below (1,4,6,7,10, and 11), Levertov gives presence and weight to white space on the page where no words are, but where the eye and mind seem to hover, hesitating briefly to find direction. But even as the reader pauses, the frequent lack of punctuation at line's end together with an assemblage of inconclusive end-words, often articles or pronouns, pulls him forward, inviting him down to the next line for completion: "The / Mexican light"; "that / 'smells like autumn' "; "his / black gleaming fur"; "nevertheless he / keeps moving"; "approach but / not direction" (*Earlier Poems* 55). The tension of stop and start is palpable. Each pause seems to bring the reader to an edge solid enough to hold him for a moment, but which he is compelled to feel his way past cautiously before moving onward, like the "sniffing" dog, "engaged in its perceptions." Levertov is not only informing her readers about the nature of journeying, but making them feel the motion, awkward though steady, various and satisfying.

At the heart of many of the poems of these early volumes is the recognition of "what is possible" ("The

Palm Tree," *Earlier Poems* 56) in the creative response to nature's energies. Levertov sounds something like William Carlos Williams when he spoke "To a Solitary Disciple," asking him or her not to romanticize that which is seen, but to observe the drama of elemental forms, to notice not that the moon is "shell-pink" or the sky "is smooth / as a turquoise," but:

> how the dark
> converging lines
> of the steeple
> meet at the pinnacle—
>
> . . . .
> . . . observe
> the oppressive weight
> of the squat edifice![16]

Thus Levertov reminds her readers that

> there are no miracles but facts.
> To see! (there might be work
>   a challenge, a poem)
>
> The squat palm!
>   ("The Palm Tree," *Earlier Poems* 56)

And yet she recognizes, too, that such realization is linked to the poet's attraction to a wilder magical nature, which, engaging the imagination that is "eager, eager, for the fabulous / poem," heightens the senses, marking the way finally for clear vision

BEGINNINGS

> . . . only after the wind
> is quenched
> the tree dull
> a quietness come
> does the scraping mind perceive
> > what is possible:
> there are no miracles but facts (56).

Though refusal to see the "object" for itself is falsification, the impact of the poem lies not only in this knowledge but in the imaginative portrait that precedes it of what is *im*possible: "The bright moon stranded like a whale"; "the mistral furious / out of the back hills seawards in black flames"; and "the mule-eared palm," "quickened" to a "frenzy" with the storm (*Earlier Poems* 55). This is sight with the inner rather than the outward eye, setting the mind "agape," and "scavenging" (56) for meaning beyond the moment. Though Levertov renounces such frantic seeking, the creative presentation of her doing so suggests that the plain object is enlivened by the metaphorizing imagination. The mysterious power of "The Palm Tree" is recognizable in its squat stolidity precisely because it has been revealed against the whirligig confusions of the storm scene which serve as a perceptual backdrop.

"Silence / surrounds the facts. A language / still unspoken," Levertov declares early ("A Silence," *Earlier Poems* 35). It is the poet's task in response to offer "acts of language," "a hope, man-made" that is "counter to 'unlived life'" ("Ink Drawings" 39). Like a poet to whom she pays "Homage," who is "listening / to the crash and

sighing, crash / and sighing dance of the words" (42) in
the sounds of the world he inhabits, Levertov in these
early poems discovers appropriate language to explore
the range of her experience. She examines the simplest
actions like "Laying the Dust":

> What a sweet smell rises
>   when you lay the dust—
> bucket after bucket of water thrown
> on the yellow grass (48).

And she explores complex relationships that entangle
human lives ("The Marriage" 47). Levertov finds descriptive voice to present both exotic and fairly familiar
places ("A Supermarket in Guadalajara, Mexico" 70;
"Merritt Parkway" 60) and intensely personal voice to
mourn a father's dying, but not the death of love:

>   I dance
> for joy, only for joy
> while you lie dying, into whose eyes
> I looked seldom enough, all the years,
> seldom with candid love. Let my dance
> be mourning then,
> now that I love you too late.
>
>   ("In Obedience" 67–68)

Despite the directness of her response to her immediate environment, Levertov's voice is also shaped by
the narrative structures of myth, folk and fairy tale,
family memories, histories, and legends, that are an important part of many of her verses. In "The Earthwo-

man and the Waterwoman" she offers simple, almost stark, physical description with sudden twists of phrase and fact that turn commonplace story into myth. Thus, the description of one woman "by her oven" who "tends her cakes of good grain," is transformed by the poet's direct identification of her with extrahuman objects and energies: she "has oaktree arms"; "Her children / [are] full of blood and milk"; when she "has had her fill of the good day" and "curls to sleep in her warm hut," her rest is a well-earned, satisfying and delicious "dark fruitcake sleep." Her counterpart who "sings gay songs in a sad voice" has "moonshine children" and effectively awakens to the magic of her fragile but wondrous life when the other sleeps: "the waterwoman / goes dancing in the misty lit-up town / in dragonfly dresses and blue shoes" (*Earlier Poems* 31–32).

This is a brief generalized tale of elemental women. One is a being of the day, pursuing domestic duties, solid and steady, physical, direct, a doer, the other is a spirit of night and moonlight, mercurial, emotional, a dancer and singer. Though marked by the passage of time (from waking to sleep, day to night), the narrative functions essentially outside of place and time, existing as much for what it represents as for what it is. It reveals in its carefully rendered archetypal figures the separate strengths and impulses that together comprise a whole woman. Levertov's creative life as revealed in her poems, both early and late, is a response to these opposites—often a reconciliation and merging of them, sometimes, in difficult conflict, a choice between them.

The capacity for reconciliation, and the path to it laid out in these first books, comes in part from the experience of the family and ancestral inheritance. The instant Levertov comes to know her mother's pleasure in the natural world, the world of the senses, and to recognize her mother's excitement before the romantic world of myth and the rich language of her native Wales, she begins to know herself better. She is awakened by the charged moment, stirred by the foreign sound of "Eryri" which her mother, looking up while gathering mushrooms with her daughter, unthinkingly exclaims, rather than the literary English name, "Snowdon".

> 'Look!' she grips me, 'It is
>   Eryri!
>   It's Snowdon, fifty
>   miles away!'—the voice
> a wave rising to Eryri,
> falling.
>
> ("The Instant," *Earlier Poems* 66)

Here is the "home / of eagles, resting place of / Merlin, core of Wales," at the inherited center of the poet's connection with the spirit of a larger world of experience. Levertov carries the moment of discovery in memory, sounding and seeing clearly both the natural objects that comprised the physical scene and the stirring romance of the mountain shrouded in mystery. She recalls and envisions not only "Mushrooms firm, cold; / tussocks of dark grass, gleam of webs, / turf soft and cropped. Quiet and early," but also "Light" that "graces the mountainhead / for a lifetime's look, before the mist draws in again" (66).

"My parents," Levertov writes, "were exotic birds in the plain English coppice of Ilford, Essex . . . he a converted Russian Jew who, after spending the First World War teaching at the University of Leipzig . . . settled in England and was ordained as a priest of the Anglican Church; she a Welshwoman who had grown up in a mining village and later in a North Wales country town, and subsequently travelled widely."[17] Her father's Hasidic ancestry, an inheritance of common sense, scholarship, and mysticism, strongly marked her thought and sensibility, while her "mother's very strong sense of history" stirred her to look past the surfaces of things, "seeking-out and exploring" as a child, for instance, "the vanishing traces of the village Ilford which London had engulfed."[18] Too, her mother's keen awareness of the senses and her appreciation of life stirring around her taught the daughter "to watch the sublime metamorphoses / unfold and unfold / over the walled back gardens of our street" ("The 90th Year," *Life* 24).

From one of her "Illustrious Ancestors," Rabbi Shneur Zalman, the famous "Rav / of Northern White Russia," whose deeds and tales were not only told to the family by her father, but recorded in philosopher Martin Buber's encyclopedic *Tales of the Hasidim: The Early Masters*, Levertov learned the importance of directness in communication and action. As the story which the poet quotes in verse is retold by Buber, "The rav once asked his son: 'What do you pray with?' The son understood the meaning of the question, namely on what he based his prayer. He answered: 'With the verse: "Every stature shall prostrate itself before thee." ' Then he asked his father: 'And with what do you pray?' He said: 'With the floor and the bench.' "[19]

The literalist lesson suggests not only the importance of concrete action before abstract reasoning, but invites the reader to recognize that acts of attention are crucial if one is to understand another. The message that it is essential to listen, to pay attention, after all, to the full range of experience around one, even though one is firmly and properly committed to well-defined goals, is expanded and reiterated in another Zalman tale which Levertov weaves into her poem.

Rabbi Pinhas wanted to teach [Zalman] the language of birds and the language of plants, but the younger man refused. "There is only *one* thing men need understand," he said.
In his old age, Rabbi Shneur Zalman was once driving through the country with his grandson. Birds were hopping about and twittering everywhere. The rabbi put his head out of the carriage for awhile. "How fast they chatter," he said to the child. "They have their own alphabet. All you need do is listen and grasp well, and you will understand their language."[20]

As Levertov puts it in her poem, the Rav "used / what was at hand—as did / Angel Jones of Mold," her other "Illustrious Ancestor" "whose meditations / were sewn into coats and britches" (*Earlier Poems* 77), a "tailor, teacher, and preacher, to whom Daniel Owen, 'the Welsh Dickens' was apprenticed" (*Light* 238). As inheritor, taking life from them while imaginatively and interpretively breathing life into their stories, "thinking some line still taut between me and them," Levertov "would like to make"

> poems direct as what the birds said,
> hard as a floor, sound as a bench,
> mysterious as the silence when the tailor
> would pause with his needle in the air.
>
> (*Earlier Poems* 78)

In "Scenes from the Life of the Peppertrees," perhaps the most suggestive and accomplished poem in her early books, Levertov composes verse direct enough yet mysterious enough in its sounds and silences to tighten firmly her connection to the ancestral lines. The poem begins with an immediate but ambiguous exclamation: "The peppertrees, the peppertrees!" (*Earlier Poems* 72). Because there is no context and no directive syntax, the reader cannot be sure what is expected of him in these opening lines. He is asked to observe the trees, but with what recognition? If he is to feel excited, as the punctuation seems to suggest, he cannot help but wonder why. What is unusual about *these* trees? Or if he is to feel anxiety, as if the exclamation is a warning of some sort, what is he to watch out for? The single line stands by itself, double spaced away from the lines that follow, an emphasis demanding elaboration.

Without having directly articulated any specific questions, the poet has created both tension and confusion; yet because of the thumping emphasis of the one line, she has also left the reader feeling, almost subliminally, confident that resolution is to follow quickly. However, Levertov acts not to relieve tension but to heighten it in the next lines. Instead of further clarifying descriptions of the peppertrees, the poet offers a description, apparently unrelated to the opening, of confident cats, "sure of everything" (*Earlier Poems* 72), stretching into the new morning air. Like the cats, but sure of nothing, the reader is being stretched, waiting for some sort of completion of thought and action.

The scene unfolds itself slowly, like the gathering morning light, enacting a small drama of contrasts in the world still free of human presences save that of the observing and imagining poet. At the center of attention, dark forms and mysterious shadows play against the brightness of increasing sunshine. In their lack of clarity they create vague feelings of unease about what should be a comfortable morning moment. In part simply a precise rendering of what the eye can see in the early daylight hours, the scene of sharp juxtapositions also takes on meaning that cannot be primarily explained by the limits of the senses.

Contrasts become more surprising, more complex, and the "Scenes from the Life of the Peppertrees" begin to take on disconcerting animations. The peppertrees, knottily rooted and apparently immobile, but seeming barely attached to the scene of awakening, cast off "an air / of lightness; of shadows / scattered lightly." They "stand aside in diffidence" before the surety of the cat's and the sun's movements, and "shiver a little" (*Earlier Poems* 72) in their own insubstantiality, shaken, perhaps, by a jump of the "Robust / and soot-black" cat or by the unseen wind or, strangely and magically, by an anticipation of some tension or crisis. The simpler explanations are both affirmed and offset by the observation that "the cat / leaps to a low branch. Leaves / close about him." The cat, moving into the tree, seems to be swallowed by it whole, as if in completion of some Darwinian act. Lines in the next stanza suggest even more mysteriously that the identities of cat and tree have merged, each taking energy and identity from the other, as the poet now sees "Shadows of cats / weave round the tree trunks, / the exposed knotty roots" (73). Contraries, while not denied, are somewhat reconciled, nature's reciprocity affirmed.

As if in partial explanation of the poem's mystery, Levertov has said that in " 'Scenes from the Life of the Peppertrees' some fragment of buried myth seems to appear" (*Poet* 71). The meaning is never wholly revealed but is perhaps most suggestively raised in the poem's final stanza which opens with the missing human presence restored at last. Moving from outside to inside in this morning scene, Levertov's readers observe "The man on the bed sleeping / defenseless" (*Earlier Poems* 73). The matter of fact use of the definite article—"the" man, instead of the more general "a" man—seems to suggest that even though they have not yet encountered

him in the poem, they know him, expect him. His soli-
tariness and vulnerability are poignantly caught in details of his physique and position:

> his bare long feet together
> sideways, keeping each other
> warm. And the foreshortened shoulders,
> the head
> barely visible (73).

"He is good," the poet concludes, "let him sleep." But
the third peppertree, uneasily rooted no longer, catlike
and perhaps having taken boldness from the cat or perhaps simply moved by its own force, "restless, twitch-
ing / thin leaves in the light / of afternoon" will not let
innocence rest.

> After a while
> it walks over and taps
> on the upstairs window with a bunch
> of red berries. Will he wake? (73)

The attempted awakening may suggest homage to the
sleeper, an offering of a natural bounty of red berries to
innocence and goodness. Or it may suggest danger or
threat, some action of the cat-devouring tree. Too, the
different possibilities may merge, suggesting the risk in
disturbing goodness, whatever the reason.

Appropriately, the poem which has offered suggestive possibilities rather than answers ends inconclu-
sively, with a question which invites another. To the
extent that the sleeper is a "man" he must, of course,

awaken sometime. But will he wake to this summoning? And if he does, what will he be awakening to? If not, when and under what circumstances will he shake off slumbers? The reader is left to ponder the future of sleeping goodness and its relation to the world of nature. In representing a scene in the natural world even while transforming it into myth, giving a surprising sentience to the tree and archetypal breadth to the human, Levertov has brought her readers closer to the mysteries that link this world with others.

With Eyes at the Back of Our Heads (1960), the final and most ambitious of what can properly be called Levertov's early books, seems both to sum up and enlarge the measure of her poetic growth and achievement over more than a decade. "Incise, invent, file to poignance," her speaker advises in the final stanza of the book's penultimate poem:

> make your elusive dream
>   seal itself
> in the resistant mass of crude substance.

> ("Art," *Eyes* 73)

And the book shows the way, mingling dream with the commonplace, myth and meditation with the immediate, forms with experience, things as they are and as they might be.

The title poem, a teasing blend of direct statement, comfortingly familiar fairy-tale structures and events, and suddenly disconcerting logic-defying transformations, marks out the landscape and mindscape of the poet's imaginative terrain. "With eyes at the back of our heads" is a phrase the reader recognizes as cliché, one that invites him even before he has read a line to expect a set of standard meanings and associations. With such eyes he might protect himself, seeing dangers or challenges that otherwise would come upon him unawares. Or, able to see in unexpected directions, he might better handle the chaos that surrounds him in his busy and crowded life even as he perceives the tasks that lie before him. Less literally, the reader might perceive the path he has followed, his past as it gives way to and shapes his future. But though these expected meanings, never fully dismissable once raised, linger to add a dimension of significance as he reads, they remain essentially a measure of how inadequate the typical and received meanings may be once worked upon by the shaping imagination.

For Levertov is writing less about the idea of heightened external sight than about inner vision. "With eyes at the back of our heads" we see not necessarily more simply or clearly but more hopefully and inventively. The reader does not fix upon obstacles, as he might with his sense-locked eyes, rather he sees possibilities, albeit puzzling ones. He is better able to recognize and imagine essential interrelationships, and thereby may begin to "Set . . . to rights" the "imperfect" structures of the experiences he seeks (*Eyes* 9).

The poem begins as if in the middle of a journey with familiar landmarks of folk and fairy tales: a distant mountain, a shifting landscape, a mysterious "knitter" who can thread together a magical garment that will clear the way. But despite the signposts, much is confused. For Levertov offers not the logic of any simple literary genre, even one as fluid as fairy-tale narrative. Rather, seeking both to demonstrate and explain the workings of the imagination, she deliberately presents fragments of logic and insight, leaps of mercurial imagining. Making sense, but never completely, the abrupt juxtapositions of image and event dislocate the reader, immersing him in a journey into places behind the eye, which, though felt and thereby comprehended as experience, cannot be completely understood.

With the "eyes at the back of our heads," the speaker declares, we do not perceive our paths blocked, our journeys prohibitively difficult or impossible to complete, however hard the travels: "we see a mountain / not obstructed with woods but laced / here and there with feathery groves" (*Eyes* 9). Levertov's travelers face the uncertainty of their own confused perceptions and desires, of not knowing exactly what lies before them, as the mountain they have reached seems suddenly to have doors, to be a house, or perhaps just a facade:

> The doors before us in a facade
> that perhaps has no house in back of it
> are too narrow, and one is set high
> with no doorsill. . . .
>
> . . . .
> For we want
> to enter the house, if there is a house,
> to pass through the doors at least
> into whatever lies beyond them . . . (9).

But with a kind of dreamlike logic of inward sight, the travelers are able to recognize and accept the radical perceptual transformations which can bring them to their goal. It takes a shaper, in this case a "knitter," to turn things to right, making of the rigid door, which may front on no house, leading nowhere, a garment, something to put on, not pass through:

> The architect sees

> > the imperfect proposition and
> > turns eagerly to the knitter.
> > Set it to rights!
> > The knitter begins to knit (9).

Using the imagination, each participant in the journey must accept the flexibility of a reciprocal relationship. He must take shape from and give shape to the objects that stand on his experiential path, rather than seeking to impose a restricting structure upon them:

> > For we want
> > to enter the house, if there is a house,
> > . . . .
> > we want to enter the arms
> > of the knitted garment. As one
> > is re-formed, so the other,
> > in proportion.

> > > > > > > (*Eyes* 9)

"When the doors widen / when the sleeves admit us," the speaker informs the reader, "the way to the mountain will clear." And sight will be sharp with precise physical details, insight rich with evocative visions: "green, mountain / cut of limestone, echoing / with hidden rivers, mountain / of short grass and subtle shadows" (*Eyes* 9, 10).

Although the imagination swims below the surfaces of things, "shining dark-scaled fish, / swims and waits, flashes, waits and / wavers, shining of its own light" ("The Lagoon," *Eyes* 16), Levertov insists that art be active and challenging. The artist must not wait but must draw light up from the inner recesses and "learn to see again, / construct, break through / to 'the thrill of continuance with the appearance of all its changes' " ("Art," *Eyes* 72). "Wear scarlet!" she admonishes, "Tear the green lemons / off the tree!   I don't want / to forget who I am, what has burned in me / and hang limp and clean, an empty dress" ("The Five-Day Rain," *Eyes* 13). But the risk is not simply an emptying, a loss of creative and energetic self; it is yielding to complacency. As a reminder, proscription, and antidote, Levertov offers the parable of "The Goddess" (*Eyes* 43). Levertov writes that the poem "in which a goddess who is truth tosses the protagonist out of 'Lie Castle' " takes its energy "from an experience of awakening to the truth and to the necessity for truthfulness" (*Poet* 72). More self-consciously didactic than many of Levertov's early poetic narratives, and therefore more efficiently schematic, the poem nonetheless is enriched by an unpredictable mixture of expressive modes which actively engages the reader. The poem is not only received as a message, but is felt as experience, constantly changing and often mysterious.

Even the progress of the didactic allegorical narrative that begins the poem is surprising. What seems direct statement, an explanation of the relationship of the protagonists that will convey the message about the nature of creativity, quickly gains an unexpected form. Levertov opens simply with straight forward narration:

> She in whose lipservice
> I passed my time,
> whose name I knew, but not her face,
> came upon me where I lay in Lie Castle!
>
> (*Eyes* 43)

But rather than a sober drama built upon a serious introduction, Levertov presents action that slips into almost cartoonlike gestural violence:

> [She] Flung me across the room, and
> room after room (hitting the walls, re-
> bounding—to the last
> sticky wall—wrenching away from it
> pulled hair out!)
> till I lay
> outside the outer walls! (43)

Of course the suggestion is clear that each and every lie (room) in the house of deception must be met with bruising directness if one is to break free successfully from the self-destructive confines of falsehood. But the message is disarming, delivered so broadly with exaggerated "bounding" comic-strip visual and sonic energy. The reader is struck by the message, but bemused as well by its delivery. Surprised and off balance rather than nodding sagely, he awaits with uncertainty the progress toward dramatic and didactic denouement. What follows changes pace again, and the reader, unable to settle into predictable patterns of recognition, attends to the experience being revealed.

When the scene shifts from the once cozy but dangerously entrapping interior to the exposed but promising exterior, from the "sticky wall" of Lie Castle to the "cold air" "outside the outer walls," the action is less physical, the language more richly metaphoric and magical. While a single onomatopoetic flourish serves as a lingering echo of the broad gestural drama of the fight scene, "I tasted the mud that splattered my lips" (43), Levertov turns from the violence of separation to the mystery of discovery that accompanies change. After the near caricature of the early action which kept the reader observant but emotionally disengaged, the images of new creativity seem exciting. Engaging the reader fully now while continuing to prevent complacencies of comprehension, Levertov collapses boundaries of space and place, putting the emphasis in this didactic drama clearly on the wonder of new possibilities rather than on the limits of old mistakes.

New life springs up in the unprotected natural terrain that confronts one after separation from familiar but false security: "I tasted the mud . . . / the seeds of a forest were in it, / asleep and growing!" Here where one cannot hide behind walls of one's own constructing, where one must be aware of and responsive to elemental forces, creative silences are finally answered by new voice:

> The silence was answering my silence,
> a forest was pushing itself
> out of sleep between my submerged fingers.
>
> I bit on a seed and it spoke on my tongue.
>
> *(Eyes* 43)

The true voice, the Goddess', lodged in the poet's throat, speaks to us not of "close rooms" (44) or of the elaborate pomp of man-made forms built like ponderous castles, but of renewals in nature, of organic interrelationships that interfuse sky and ground, water and wind. These cannot be controlled by men, but may be perceived and represented by the power of the responsive imagination:

> . . . a seed . . . spoke on my tongue
> of day that shone already among stars
> in the water-mirror of low ground,
> and a wind rising ruffled the lights:
> she passed near . . .
> she who plucked me from the close rooms,
>
> without whom nothing
> flowers, fruits, sleeps in season,
> without whom nothing
> speaks in its own tongue, but returns
> lie for lie! (43–44)

BEGINNINGS

Levertov's "truths" in *With Eyes at the Back of Our Heads* are the often surprising truths of change and coherence, revealed in small as well as grand moments, caught in a variety of forms. In a brief descriptive lyric, the poet's close observation of white butterflies "Everywhere among the marigolds / the rainblown roses and the hedges / of tamarisk," shows "whiteness" to be only an illusion of the "constant / tremulous movement" ("The Dead Butterfly"). Stilled in death, the butterfly is "traced with green," not fragile, but resembling "the stones / of which the city is built, / quarried high in the mountains" (*Eyes* 14). Too, a number of self-centering mediations define the "Pleasures" of recognizing the vitality hidden unexpectedly in the patterns and contradictions of the commonplace:

> I like to find
> what's not found
> at once, but lies
>
> within something of another nature,
> in repose, distinct (17).

It is to be seen in the small and quiet discovery of

> . . . the juicy stem of grass that grows
> within the coarser leaf folded round,
> and the butteryellow glow
> in the narrow flute from which the morning-glory
> opens blue and cool on a hot morning (17–18).

And it is felt in the noise and throb of a "February Evening in New York," "the multiple disordered tones / of gears changing, a dance / to the compass points" which, flowing out over the "Prospect of sky / wedged into avenues, left at the ends of streets, / west sky, east sky," suggests "more life tonight! A range / of open time at winter's outskirts" (31).

But always the center of the search for truth in *With Eyes at the Back of Our Heads* lies in Levertov's penchant for making and remaking myths. This is not the encoding of knowledge that critic Elizabeth Sewell described as *"cipher"* in *The Orphic Voice*, a book that Levertov knew well. As Sewell wrote, a situation in which *"'This stands for that' . . . is cipher and not myth."*[21] Levertov presents, rather, an immediate identification of disparate objects and experiences, one linked inseparably with another and perceived as fused, however unusual the connections might seem. She is interested in what American poet Hart Crane called the play of "illogical impingements of words on the consciousness."[22]

Thus in a mythic re-creation of "Xochipilli" (*Eyes* 66), the pre-Columbian God of Spring who "creates red flowers from the dung of a serpent that coils and preens in the heart of a fire in the God's hearth" and makes "white flowers from the bones of small animals, sacrificed to serve as food for the snake" (*Poet* 73), Levertov creates an immediate evocation of the spirit of the natural world where transformations make sense beyond the rational, and nature's rhythms and sounds transfer energy to one another in a cycle of creative renewal.

BEGINNINGS

> Rain dances many-footed
> on the thatch. Raindrops
> leap into the fire, the serpent hisses.
>
> "From this music
> seeds of the grass
> that shall sing when the wind blows."
>
> *(Eyes* 66)

From such music, interfusing magic and sensory experience, creation and observation, Levertov takes the theme and shape of what is perhaps the most original poem in the book, her complex serial verse, "A Ring of Changes" *(Eyes* 37). "There is a long history in each one of us," William Carlos Williams has written, "that comes as not only a reawakening but a repossession when confronted by this world."[23] The six linked parts of "A Ring of Changes" reveal the nature of "this world" and Levertov's intensely personal "repossession" of it. Yet the opening sections of the poem seem to avoid typical syntax and the use of active verbs that would set the frame for narrative or would suggest that the subject involves an action that moves through time toward some completion. The opening begins, rather, as if to create a series of impressions of immediate experience.

Though obviously concerned philosophically with time, with endings and new starts, the initial descriptions of "autumn seeds" and other marks of cyclical change are rendered free of distinction between subject and object, thing acting or thing acted upon. As a result, the reader first encounters, not the directive mind of a dramatic narrator, but the seemingly unmediated scene itself. No persona describes the exact relationship between "Shells, husks" and the "autumn seeds" that are "wandering," or explains that "curled indoor leaves" loiter, and hold "many days before falling." The scene simply unfolds itself, a list of uncompleted but continuing happenings, one juxtaposed with another:

> Shells, husks, the wandering
> of autumn seeds, the loitering
> of curled indoor leaves . . .
>
> . . . .
> Cracking husk, afraid
> it may reveal a dirty emptiness
>
> . . . .
> bitter, of no account.

(Eyes 37)

By the end of the poem's first stanzas, however, as if drawn forth by the unemphatic pace of natural change, agitated by its randomness, by the waiting that seems almost to proclaim a reluctance to change or a fear of altered states, a new impatient tone is sounded. As if propelled by an urgent need to participate in the experience of natural change and to ensure its happening, a personal voice intrudes issuing directives, a list of imperatives to stamp the individual will on the "wandering," "loitering," desultory scene:

> Seed, cling
> to the hard earth, some footstep
> will grind you in,

> new leaf, open your green hand,
> old leaf, fall and rot
> enriching your rich brotherhood,
>
> hazelnut, know when ripeness
> has . . . sweetened you.
>
> (*Eyes* 37)

The urgency, initially a bit perplexing after the leisurely opening, makes sense less in the context of the natural cycles that seem to have called it forth, than in relation to the intense self-observations and revelations that follow in stanza after stanza. For the reader quickly discovers that the poem is less about natural than personal change, and the experience of seasonal renewal is but a prologue and touchstone to explorations of the speaker's individual doubt and hope for renewal.

As the seed must slough off the husk in order to renew itself, so the speaker in section 2 acknowledges the need to shuck off self-protective surfaces, "To shed this fake face / as a snakeskin" (*Eyes* 37). But she acknowledges, too, the pain of such a step and the rationalizations marshaled by the reluctant mind to prevent it:

> to dig shame up, a buried bone
> and tie it to my breast—
>
> (would it change, in time
> to an ornament? Could it serve
> to be carved with new designs?) (38)

Levertov moves her reader closer to the heart of the matter in section 3 with another look inward at the dangerous and potentially isolating nature of pursuit of change measured now in terms of personal relationships:

> our dreams move together
> in our dark heads, wander
> in landscapes unlit by our candle eyes
> eyes of self love and self disgust
> eyes of your love for me kindling my cold heart
> eyes of my love for you flickering at the edge of you.
>
> (*Eyes* 38)

By contrast, in section 4, Levertov offers a brief poignant summary, loving and regretful, of the perhaps inevitable risks and results of ceasing to seek change, even in old age:

> *Among the tall elders of the hereafter*
> *my father had become*
> >   *a blissful foolish rose*
> *his face beaming from among petals*
> *(of sunset pink) "open as a daisy"—*
> *a rose walking, tagging at the heels*
> *of the wise, having found*
> *a true form.*
>
> (*Eyes* 39)

With the poem's first four sections having awakened both speaker and readers to the implications of the range of experience of change, the last two take them to the deep center of both the potential and the pain of the impulse. The reader discovers that in the speaker's house "The tree of life is growing / in a corner of the living-room." Free to respond to the potentially nurturing environment, it is "held to its beam by nails / that encircle, not pierce, its stem" and stirs to the notes of a man-made music that fills the room. The silent, living wood is quickened by contraries, by the transformation of sound wrought upon the cut and shaped wood of the "hollow" cello:

> Casal's cello (a live broadcast: the resistances
> of the live bow, the passion manifest
> in living hands, not smoothed out on wax)
> speaks from across the room
> and the tree of life answers. . . .

(Eyes 39)

While "Cello and vine commune / in the space of a room" (*Eyes* 41), their harmonies marked "As bow touches strings," and "a path / moves toward a leaf," the human listener realizes a failure of communication:

> There is space in us
>
> but the lines and planes of its form
> are what we reach for and fall,
> touching nothing . . .
> . . . .
> Buds are knots in our flesh, nodules of pain (40).

It is a pain exacerbated, not only by the failure of dynamic relationship, but of creativity for the speaker and a companion who seem to be defined in part by an art they seek to make but who are drawing only on an "immeasurable [internal] darkness" (40) in an effort to give form to experience:

> What will speak to you?
> What notes of abundance
> strike across the living room
> to your bowed head and down-curved back?
> . . . .
> Listen, listen . . .
> We are in this room
> together. You are alone
> forming darkness into words
> dark on white paper,
> I am alone with the sense of your anguish (41).

Yet in awareness of the pain of growth, of recognition of potential for change, there is promise. "The tree of life," after all, "is growing in the room, / the livingroom, the work-room" (*Eyes* 41), and its perceivable health suggests that if one is not perpetually and self-protectively on guard against change, one may awaken instinctively to dispel the dark at the center of entrapping isolation and immobility:

> From the doorway we saw
> harmonies and heard
> measured colors of light, not quite awake and so awake
> to correspondences. A room in a house in the city
> became for a space of fine, finely-drawn,
> November morning, a Holy Apple Field (42).

Attuned to the music of contrasts and correspondences here as throughout Levertov's first four volumes, the reader watches with the speaker and her companion as light and energy "[fill] unpeopled space with presence" (*Eyes* 41), drawing the vine "Green to the white ceiling" (42). In this longest poem of her own first period of major growth and change, Levertov comes finally to an affirmation of hope that is "an awareness involving the whole self, a *knowing* . . . a 'being in touch' " (*Poet* 54). In the next decade of her poetic journey this hope would be tried and tested repeatedly in even more deeply personal ways and in the public forum.

Notes

1. Kenneth Rexroth, "The New Poetry," *Assays* (New York: New Directions, 1961) 189.

2. Charles Olson, "Projective Verse," *Selected Writings of Charles Olson*, ed., introd., Robert Creeley (New York: New Directions, 1966) 16, 19.

3. Ezra Pound, *Gaudier-Brzeska* (New York: New Directions, 1970) 110.

4. William Carlos Williams, *The Autobiography of William Carlos Williams* (New York: New Directions, 1951) 264–65.

5. Levertov, "A Poet's View," *Religion and Intellectual Life* 1 (Summer 1984): 51.

6. Levertov, "A Poet's View" 52–53.

7. Levertov, "A Poet's View" 52.

8. Kenneth John Atchity, "An Interview with Denise Levertov," *San Francisco Review of Books*, March, 1979: 6.

9. Atchity, "Interview" 8.

10. Reid, " 'Everyman's Land': Ian Reid Interviews Denise Levertov," *Southern Review* (Adelaide, Australia) 5 (1972): 233.

11. Reid, "Everyman's Land" 235–36.

12. Muriel Rukeyser, introductory note to *The Life of Poetry* N. pag.

13. Walter Sutton, "A Conversation with Denise Levertov," *The Minnesota Review* 5 (1965): 335.

14. Reid, "Everyman's Land" 234.

15. Levertov, "The Ideas in the Things" 131.

16. William Carlos Williams, *Selected Poems* (New York: New Directions, 1969) 10–11.

17. Levertov, "Denise Levertov Writes," *The Bloodaxe Book of Contemporary Women Poets: Eleven British Writers*, ed. Jeni Couzyn (Newcastle-upon-Tyne: Bloodaxe, 1985) 75.

18. Levertov, "Denise Levertov Writes" 76.

19. Martin Buber, *Tales of the Hasidim: The Early Masters* (New York: Schocken, 1947) 269. My discussion draws upon Ronald Younkins, "Denise Levertov and the Hasidic Tradition," *Descant* 19 (Fall 1974): 40–48. While Buber spells Zalman's name "Shneur," Levertov spells it "Schneour." I follow Buber's spelling here.

20. Buber, 266–67.

21. Sewell as quoted in Denise Levertov, *The Poet in the World* (New York: New Directions, 1973) 57.

22. Hart Crane, "A Discussion with Hart Crane," *Poetry; A Magazine of Verse* 29 (1926): 36, quoted in Philip Wheelwright, *The Burning Fountain: A Study in the Language of Symbolism*, new and revised ed. (Bloomington: Indiana University Press, 1968) 47.

23. Williams, *Autobiography* 19.

CHAPTER THREE

Discoveries and Explorations:
The Jacob's Ladder, O Taste and See,
The Sorrow Dance

"Insofar as poetry has a social function it is to awaken sleepers by other means than shock" (*Poet* 3), Levertov wrote in a now well-known testimony for Donald M. Allen's 1960 anthology *The New American Poetry.* Clarifying in 1973, she added: "I was talking about form, not content. . . . I was deploring shock as an end in itself, while espousing the act of 'awakening sleepers' as a goal (not *the* goal) proper to poetry. Today I would stand by the concept, still, that poetry's social function is such an act. . . . The poem has a social *effect* of some kind whether or not the poet wills that it have. It has kinetic force" (5–6).

Her "exploratory" kinetic work of the 1960s which she came to call "organic poetry" (*Poet* 7) sought increasingly to awaken its readers, not only to social realities, but to the recognition that an outward sight necessitates an inner gaze and understanding: "There can be no self-respect without respect for others, no love and reverence for others without love and reverence for oneself" (53). As she put it years later:

Goethe said, 'In order to *do* something one has to *be* someone.' He was not talking about status and power (or rather not about the power of status). He was talking about the necessity for self-development, for individuation, as a vital accompaniment to effective action. . . . I feel strongly that internal work and external work, the self-directed or introspective and the publicly-directed, must be concurrent, or at least rhythmically alternating. They are complementary, and neither can be substituted for the other (*Light* 95–96).

Levertov's inward and outward directed verses were energized by friendship and exchange of ideas with Robert Creeley and Robert Duncan, whom Levertov thought of in 1959 as "the chief poets among my contemporaries" (*Poet* 3), by her reading of Charles Olson's work, and, especially, by continued delight in, and attention to, the writings of Williams and Rilke.

"Form," Creeley had announced, "is never more than the extension of content." At a Vancouver poetry conference in the summer of 1963 Levertov proposed to Creeley that the dictum should be changed to read: "'Form is never more than the *revelation* of content.'—(to which he agreed)" (*Poet* 60). But form and its relationship to content may be neither simple nor straightforward. As she learned "from Duncan more than from anyone else . . . there must be a place in the poem for rifts too. . . . Great gaps between perception and perception which must be leapt across if they are to be crossed at all." This was a view that challenged Charles

DISCOVERIES AND EXPLORATIONS

Olson and Edward Dahlberg's "law" of "Projective Verse" that "one perception must immediately and directly lead to a further perception" (13).[1] "Duncan," she remembered in 1975, "often sounded for me a note of 'permission' to my native eclecticism that some shyness in me, some lack of self-confidence, longed for" (*Light* 211). Perhaps most important, her supportive literary friendships encouraged her to continue to explore and affirm the view "that language, as Robert Duncan has declared, is not a set of counters to be manipulated, but a Power. And only in this knowledge does [the poet] arrive at music. . . . Writing poetry is a process of discovery, revealing *inherent* music, the music of correspondences, the music of inscape" (*Poet* 54).

"Those who . . . like Creeley and like myself," Levertov told her readers in a 1965 *Virginia Quarterly Review* essay, "are interested in discovering the 'inscape' of experience—the form and pattern inherent in it—regard the accurate notation of thought and feeling-patterns, in line breaks and other pauses in the poem, as a positive value. Often such pauses—counterpointing the syntactic pauses—imply the unspoken question to which the next word is the answer" (*Light* 55). In her new book of the new decade, *The Jacob's Ladder* (1961), Levertov discovered and explored in line, rhythm, and image, the forms, techniques, and subjects appropriate to her widening and deepening range of poetic experience.

The book's last poem, and its first, provide a sharp outline of the formal and thematic directions Levertov's work was taking early in the 1960s. Seeking to discover and explore what it means to be an individual and what it means to live in the world, Levertov offers a glimpse of "A Solitude" (*Ladder* 68) and of "A Common Ground" (1) and compels her readers to recognize that these are not as disparate as they might appear. As she has written elsewhere, "The self will surely suffer if egotism leads a person away from the experience of the Human Community. And the commonweal, as surely, suffers if those who work for its betterment are hollowed-out self-neglecters" (*Light* 96).

Interested in revealing "the *process* of thinking/ feeling, feeling/thinking, rather than focusing more exclusively on its *results*" as she examines the relation of self to world, Levertov finds that her "crucial precision for creating this . . . mode is the linebreak," which can rhythmically record brief pauses among perceptions:

Regular punctuation is a part of regular sentence structure, that is, of the expression of completed thoughts. . . . But in poems one has the opportunity . . . to make manifest, by an intrinsic structural means, the interplay or counterpoint of process and completion—in other words, to present the dynamics of perception *along with* its arrival at full expression. The linebreak is a form of punctuation *additional* to the punctuation that forms part of the logic of completed thoughts (*Light* 62).

The brief narrative of "A Solitude," describing the poet's encounter with a blind man on the subway, is neither about absence of vision nor "solitude." Rather it concerns that aspect of human relationship which Rilke once explained as "the mutual bordering and guarding of . . . solitudes." As Levertov came to see, "solitude, and the individual development for which it is a condition" provide "the only valid ground on which communion of the many, the plural Other of brother-and-sisterhood, can take place" (*Light*, 286).[2]

Syntax is strained throughout the poem by line-endings, rest stops that momentarily isolate units of thought, feeling, or perception for the reader's contemplation before combining into larger units of observation. Discrete impressions are never lost in a final gestalt. As Levertov seems to suggest both with her subject and her technique of presentation, any idea of wholeness must take into account the variety and complexity of the relationships of the individual parts.

The poem begins not with a simple sentence that establishes coherent structure, but with a series of fragments unraveling structure, revealing its various lines of interconnection:

> A blind man. I can stare at him
> ashamed, shameless. Or does he know it?
> No, he is in a great solitude.
>
> (*Ladder* 68)

By refusing to allow regular syntax to determine definitive meaning among several options, Levertov offers a glimpse of the nature of meaning itself—something to be assembled and reassembled by participants and observers alike, establishing relationship amidst the discrete juxtapositions that experience provides. The seemingly simple lines, demanding that the reader take an active role in making meaning, leave a variety of impressions: an ashamed speaker (nervously impolite but compelled by inner need or curiosity) stares at a blind man; a shameless speaker (protected by indifference, or by the other's failure to know) stares at a blind man; a speaker's stare, somehow unsettlingly disconnected from the rest of the speaker's self, is ashamed and / or shameless. The first line ending "him" without any punctuation, and the second beginning "ashamed, shameless," even give the reader a moment's pause to consider that the shame or lack of it is the blind man's, not the speaker's. Of course, even as he recognizes a multiplicity of meanings, the reader is discovering that some possibilities are strained, others more explicit. The opening is meant to reveal its speaker's state of mind when confronted by a situation ("a great solitude") which, promising to make few demands of self or relationship, makes many. Here with variations and leaps of logic and perception Levertov reveals the nature of "organic form."

A poem of process as well as pattern from the first, "A Solitude" continues to present and explore perceptual possibilities. Following an irregular path to meaning by moving forward and backward from ambiguous key words and line-breaks, Levertov reveals a situation filled with surprising correspondences and contraries. As the blind man "trembles" with self-absorbed motion, the train lurches into movement, "moves uptown, pulls in and / pulls out of the local stops. Within its loud / jarring movement a quiet,"

> the quiet of people not speaking,
> some of them eyeing the blind man,
> only a moment though, not thirsty like me,
>
> and within that quiet his
> different quiet, not quiet at all, a tumult
> of images, but what are his images,
>
> he is blind? He doesn't care
> that he looks strange. . . .

(*Ladder* 68)

This is a world where interiors and exteriors now reflect, now contrast with one another, where facts suddenly and surprisingly lose their assurance. Thus the phrase "he is blind?"—visually separated by a stanza break from the whole sentence to which the question mark applies ("what are his images, / he is blind?")—is perceived for a moment not as the completion of a larger question, but as a complete and distinct question in itself which directly challenges the most basic certitude of the situation (that the man on the train is blind). Further, statements are juxtaposed or broken in such a way as to render disparate meanings almost simultaneously ("he is blind? He doesn't care"; "He doesn't care / that he looks strange"). Here where interrupted definitions of self and nonself are unpredictable, we must

UNDERSTANDING DENISE LEVERTOV

take nothing for granted as we discover the many meanings of the expression, "*I am*":

> 'A nice day,
> isn't it?' says the blind man. Solitude
> walks with me, walks
>
> beside me, he is not with me, he continues
> his thoughts alone. But his hands and mine
> know one another,
>
> it's as if my hand were gone forth,
> on its own journey. I see him
> across the street, the blind man,
>
> and now he says he can find his way. He knows
> where he is going, it is nowhere, it is filled
> with presences. He says, **I am**.

(Ladder 69–70)

"Facing and communicating," Levertov's friend
Muriel Rukeyser wrote, "that will be our life, in the
world and in poetry."[3] If Levertov's presentation of the
knowledge of communication is most immediately
inner-directed in "A Solitude," a similar knowing is
more generally focused in the world in "A Common
Ground," an evocation of, and meditation upon, some
not so simple Williams-like virtues of linguistic and experiential directness.

The poet looks outward at her environment as well
as in toward her craft, hoping to plant words that will
blossom in the varied and uncompromising soil of

everyday life. She does not simply stamp patterns on diversity, but responds openly to experience as it surrounds her. Levertov seeks a language flexible enough to describe laughing girls at lunch hour, staid men "in business suits," the world of "crumpled wax-paper, cartons / of hot coffee," *and* the way "the sun's / deep tone of May gold speaks / or the spring chill in the rock's shadow" (*Ladder* 2). She follows the example of "uncommon men," poets who "have labored in their virtue / and left a store / of seeds for planting" (1). At their best, her words comprise "a language / excelling itself to be itself" (3), explicit enough to evoke desired meaning, varied enough to suggest ranges of possibility. "A Common Ground" opens with apparent declarative simplicity, identifying poetry and the poet's task in a positive way with basic activities that occur in what are sometimes unpromising environments:

> To stand on common ground
> here and there gritty with pebbles
> yet elsewhere "fine and mellow—
> uncommon fine for ploughing"
>
> there to labor
> planting the vegetable words
> diversely in their order
> that they come to virtue! (1)

But though the stanza ends with exclamatory emphasis, the lines are tense with unfinished communication as we wait for a sentence to complete itself. Though each new stanza of section one contains a coherent fragment of grammar and meaning, generally linked to lines above and below it, the pieces fail to assemble at any point into a completed semantic unit.

Thus the incomplete opening thought, "To stand on common ground," eventually gives way to "there to labor," which in turn carries the reader toward "To reach those shining pebbles," and "To crunch on words." The reader seems continually invited to ask "then what"? But instead of offering an answer, the first section carries him toward a final inconclusive ellipsis:

> To crunch on words
> grown in grit or fine
> crumbling earth, sweet
>
> to eat and sweet
> to be given, to be eaten
> in common, by laborer
> and hungry wanderer . . .

(Ladder 1)

Required to make and hold together many starts toward meaning, conceiving a variety of possible concluding "therefore clauses" as he reads, the reader is left at last with no resolving note sounded, but rather with an assemblage of vivid impressions of a writer's diverse task and terrain. The reader's understanding is both enriched and strained by the pressure of being held incomplete for so long. Stymied in any impulse to move quickly to resolution, he confronts each isolated observation with the minute attention of a seeker after order, even looping back to try to fit the growing number of pieces together, and thereby recognizing anew, time and again, the textures of each piece, "gritty" or "fine" and "shining." Levertov compels those in her audience to attend carefully to their steps as they walk and rewalk her creative ground.

As the section progresses, the sense of the "whole" becomes increasingly complex, the individual seeds of meaning more disparate; and section 2 increases the stress by piling up further fragments of observation, each simply stated but adding up to no direct, fully completed, thought. Although various parts of stanzas invite, even demand, a certain syntactic structure, the developing poem is slow to produce it. The section begins simply, "In time of blossoming, / of red / buds" (*Ladder* 1), but takes seven more descriptive lines to produce another unit of developing syntax, itself halting and interrupted: "when on the grass verges / or elephant-hide rocks, the lunch hour / expands" (2).

The awkwardness of delayed syntax may seem partially resolved by the apparent completeness of the emphatic lines that follow next: "the girls / laugh at the sun, men / in business suits awkwardly / recline" (*Ladder* 2). But the words are still governed by the initial "when" in the lines above, and the poem fails, after all, to deliver the clause invited by the implicit sentence structure. Having followed the logic despite the difficulties of having the main sentence units interrupted again and again by tension-evoking lines that stretch expectation, the reader is not offered the grammatical and semantic unit beginning with an implied or specific "then" that he has been led to expect ("In time of blossoming . . . when on the grass . . . the girls laugh" . . . then something happens). Instead, the poem's fragmented drift continues, the second section ending, too, with an ellipsis:

> human lives! Poems stirred
> into paper coffee-cups, eaten
> with petals on rye in the
> sun—the cold shadows in back,
> and the traffic grinding the
> borders of spring—entering
> human lives forever,
> unobserved, a spring element . . . (2).

By raising and frustrating linguistic and semantic expectations, challenging her readers to realize and hold partial meanings in lines that swell but won't subside, that make leaps of logic rather than steady progressions, Levertov seems to suggest that significance lies as much in the process of communication as in a final product. The impact is in what individuals experience as they make their way toward some desired or expected result, as much as in the resolution itself. That, perhaps, is the most "common ground"; and even common speech, the reader comes to realize through his participation here in the process of making meanings, of testing what he sees against what he ex-

DISCOVERIES AND EXPLORATIONS

pects, is to an extent always "uncommon," "Not . . . / a dead level" (*Ladder* 3), but unpredictable and fresh. The reader recognizes too that even sentences that do resolve more simply must still make their meanings partially as he has made his—in the gathering up of individual moments of authenticity.

Virtually all the poems of *The Jacob's Ladder* take their purpose and energy from Denise Levertov's pursuit of "The authentic" which, it seems, "rolls / just out of reach, beyond / running feet and / stretching fingers" ("Matins," *Ladder* 59), but which, in fact, lies much closer to the center of one's life. She seeks its measure "in our crowded hearts / our steaming bathrooms, kitchens full of / things to be done, the / ordinary streets" (60). And she finds that "verisimilitude draws up / heat in us, zest / to follow through" to the discovery in "joy" that authenticity is "always / a recognition, the known / appearing fully itself, and / more itself than one knew" (58, 57).

Authenticity takes shape from lives lived fully:

> Live
> in thy fingertips and in thy
>   hair's rising; hunger
>   be thine, food
>   be thine. . . .
>
>   ("Three Meditations," *Ladder* 29)

Moreover, it is visible in the fact of death faced directly and without fear:

> Darling Death
> shouted in his ear,
> . . . .
> and with that courtesy he accorded
> all clumsy living things
> that stumble in broken boots
> he bowed and
> not flinching from her black breath
> gave her his arm and walked back with her the
> way she had come and
> turned the corner.
>
> ("Deaths, *César Vallejo," Ladder* 42)

Such "Marvelous" truths, Levertov's readers discover, can "confront us / at every turn, / in every guise,
iron ball, / egg, dark horse, shadow, / cloud / of breath
on the air" ("Matins," *Ladder* 60). They dwell in the mix
of myth and memory, as the poet, poring over "A Map
of the Western Part of the County of Essex in England"
(19), recalls "a child who traced voyages / indelibly all
over the atlas":

> . . . an old
>
> map
> made long before I was born shows ancient
> rights of way where I walked when I was ten burning with
>   desire
> for the world's great splendors, a child . . .
>   . . . who now in a far country
> remembers the first river, the first
> field, bricks and lumber dumped in it ready for building,

that new smell, and remembers
the walls of the garden, the first light (20).

Perhaps most surprisingly and shockingly, these truths lie not only in recognizing what individuals were or are or may become in the ordinary worlds they inhabit daily, but in observing and acknowledging connection with what might seem completely foreign and "other." Levertov would not have her readers avoid, nor merely observe, the darkest and most distorted corners of the human experience. In a poem that represents a major breakthrough, an imaginative turning out from self so as to acknowledge the interrelationship of all individuals, Levertov presents her first work based primarily on a current and topical public event. Taking her readers to the heart of evil in "During the Eichmann Trial," she shows them a man in a glass cage:

> . . . where we may view
> ourselves, an apparition
>
> telling us something he
> does not know: we are members
>
> one of another.

> (*Ladder* 63)

"No recognition of others is possible without the imagination," Levertov wrote in 1968:

The imagination of what it is to *be* those other forms of life that want to live is the only way to recognition;

and it is that imaginative recognition that brings compassion to birth. Man's capacity for evil, then, is less a positive capacity, for all its horrendous activity, than a failure to develop man's most human function, the imagination, to its fullness, and consequently a failure to develop compassion (*Poet* 53).

In a singular effort of her own "imagination," Levertov refuses to reduce the man, Eichmann, to monster. Her portrait, horrific and unflinching, offers no shred of forgiveness. Yet she presents a comprehension which does not deny "compassion" for the human animal: "pitiful man whom none / pity, whom all / must pity if they look / into their own face" (*Ladder* 61).

An epigraph from Robert Duncan, placed at the top of the poem like an inscription above the door into the dark, suggests Levertov's concern in the lines that follow with the discoveries that are made "When we look up / each from his being" (*Ladder* 61). The poet seems to suggest that it is something not often done. The poem, entitled, not "The Eichmann Trial," but "During the Eichmann Trial," envisions concurrently what the poet sees, what the reader sees, what the man on trial sees—mingling facts and lies, memory, imagination and speculation in past time and in the present, as the public event unfolds.

The poem's first line announces "He had not looked" into himself or into those faces "seen in a lifetime." In this he is like the many who will discover something "barely known" "if they look / into their

own face (given / only by glass, steel, water . . .)," or
like "all / who look up / to see—how many / faces?"

> seen in a lifetime? (Not those
> that flash by, but those
>
> into which the gaze wanders
> and is lost
>
> and returns to tell
> **Here is a mystery,**
>
> **a person, an**
> **other, an I?**

(*Ladder* 61)

But Eichmann's "others" are the murdered
masses—"Count them. / Who are five million?" (*Ladder*
61). In an awful moment of imaginative recognition, the
poet, looking up with clear vision as the murderer
speaks, sees "a spring of blood gush from the earth—/
Earth cannot swallow / so much at once / a fountain
rushes towards the sky." The tide engulfs all, implicates
all, who cannot or will not see a self in relation to another: "Pity this man who saw it / whose obedience
continued—/ he, you, I, which shall I say?" Yet, the
poet makes clear, comprehension of human evil does
not excuse it. Eichmann's self-revealing testimony
"slur[s] into a harsh babble" as he explains himself.

In flashbacks that turn out to be foreshadowings as
well, the poet imagines revealing moments of memory

of the man who "stands / isolate in a bulletproof / witness-stand of glass" (*Ladder* 63). Using images of color to stir emotion and clarify ideas, the poet suggests that "yellow" colored the quiet moments of the childhood Eichmann remembers. "Yellow / calmed him," Levertov writes, "yellow of autumn leaves in / Wienerwald":

> yellow sun
> on the stepmother's teatable
>
> Franz Joseph's beard
> blessing his little ones (62).

But imagining this security, the poet offers imagined hints, too, of the ways it might be tied up with unpleasant emotions. The moments of yellow-tinged calm that the poet envisions, marking the child's time spent with adults in an adult world, also seem to encompass feelings of restriction and entrapment; the reader can feel the anger from it in the flat loathing of the summary "I was used from the nursery / to obedience / . . . / Corpselike / obedience" (61–62).

The meaning of the obsession with yellow—an obsession associated, perhaps, with an adult's loss of childhood security and also with resentments of the emotional cost of such secure time—expands when the reader realizes that yellow is also the color of the Star of David worn on armbands by Eichmann's victims:

> . . . the yellow
> of the stars too,

> stars that marked
> those in whose faces
>
> you had not
> looked. "They were cast out
>
> as if they were
> some animals, some beasts."
>
> (*Ladder* 62)

The color, perhaps, of the killer's love and hate, it is, Levertov reveals in part 2, most certainly a color of death.

Here, in a section whose title, "The Peachtree," offers no hint of the horror to come, Levertov imagines a single crime from accounts at the trial. Because the crime is so unspecial, it is, perhaps, more suggestive and terrible than any effort might be to summarize the enormous sweep of death. With a jarring and frightfully perverse echo of the yellow-colored recollections of the boy Eichmann, the poet describes the final days of a Jewish boy who steals a peach from Eichmann's garden and is murdered by him. Having already been compelled by the poet to glimpse the murderer's memories of childhood, the reader now stands appalled before the realization of the way the man-murderer is linked by shadowy childhood memories with the child he murders.

As the poet imagines it, the boy sees the peach,

"yellow and ripe / the vivid blood / bright in its round cheek":

> he cannot withstand desire
> it is no common fruit
>
> it holds some secret
> it speaks to the yellow star within him
>
> *(Ladder* 64)

Drawn in his "secret" difference toward the brilliant yellow as perhaps a moth is to flame, he discovers delight and death inextricably bound together: "he scales the wall / . . . / takes the peach / and death pounces" (64):

> mister death who rushes out
> from his villa
> mister death who loves yellow
>
> who wanted that yellow peach
> for himself
> mister death who signs papers
> then eats
>
> telegraphs simply: **Shoot them**
> then eats
> mister death who orders
> more transports
> then eats (64–65)

The awful repetitions gather and swell, mingling yellow and blood red in an incantation of pleasure perverted to pain and destruction that leaves the reader

DISCOVERIES AND EXPLORATIONS

drained and trembling before a madness of biblical measure:

> Son of David
> 's blood, vivid red
> and trampled juice
> yellow and sweet
> flow together beneath the tree
>
> there is more blood than
> sweet juice
> always more blood—mister
> death goes indoors
> exhausted

(Ladder 65)

The sensual immediacy of horror in section 2 anchors the confusing surreal nightmare in section 3, "Crystal Night."[4] The murder that lingers in the reader's mind, provides a reference, a particular moment of terrible awareness to help him grasp an almost incomprehensible terror which the poet presents with shards of images thrown violently together.

He is engulfed almost immediately by a phantasmagoric scene in which the explosive fears of an intolerable situation animate the inanimate:

> . . . blacked-out streets
> (wide avenues swept by curfew,
> alleyways, veins
> of dark within dark)
>
> . . . houses whose walls
> had for a long time known

> the tense stretch of skin over bone
> as their brick or stone listened. . . .
>
> *(Ladder* 66)

The city itself seems to shudder as, disembodied, "The scream! / The awaited scream rises." In a moment peace is broken, leaving "the shattering / of glass and the cracking / of bone":

> a polar tumult as when
> black ice booms, knives
> of ice and glass
> splitting and splintering the silence . . . (66).

Not yellow now, but jarring sharp contrasts of black and white fix the scene like fragments of an old newsreel rerun on a screen. The intense stress is highlighted by wrenched syntax and the choppy rhythm of short lines wedged between long ones whose assonantal and consonantal flow is abruptly interrupted. The reader is forced to watch and listen, trying like those whose fear and confusion define his perspective to make sense of the nightmare as synagogues burn, store windows break, and the Jewish population of Germany is rounded up for transportation to the death camps on November 9, 1938:

> splitting and splintering the silence into
> innumerable screaming needles of
> yes, now it is upon us, the jackboots
> are running in spurts of
> sudden blood-light through the
> broken temples

> the veils
> are rent in twain
>
> terror has a white sound
> every scream
> of fear is a white needle freezing the eyes
> the floodlights of their trucks throw
> jets of white, their shouts
> cleave the wholeness of darkness. . . .
>
> > (*Ladder* 66–67)

The shattering glass reminds Levertov's readers once again of the man isolated in the poem's present in the cagelike "witness-stand of glass" (*Ladder* 63). Having peered at him through a refracting and reflecting crystal, they finally see what they may know, or may have blocked or forgotten, but which the white scream of terror, "not / pitched in the range of common hearing," has broken free. The sound and the sights it accompanies "whistle through time"

> smashing the windows of sleep and dream
> smashing the windows of history
> a whiteness scattering
> in hailstones
> each a mirror
> for man's eyes. (67)

In the dark glass of recent history, Levertov has shown her readers an incarnation of human evil and the incomparable violence he engendered. She has shown them, too, though they may squirm and refuse the vision, a mirrored glimpse of themselves that they ignore only at their peril. As if summing up the intentions and accomplishments in *The Jacob's Ladder*, Levertov, in "Three Meditations," instructs the poet to "be with the / rivers of tumult, sharpen / thy wits to know power and be / humble" (*Ladder* 29). She must recognize, and the reader with her, that like the "Barbarians / . . . / There is darkness in me":

> I multitude, I tyrant,
> I angel, I you, you
> world, battlefield, stirring
> with unheard litanies, sounds of piercing
> green half-smothered by
> strewn bones. (30)

Ibsen has written in a passage attractive to Levertov that "The task of the poet is to make clear to *himself*, and thereby to others, the temporal and eternal questions" (*Ladder*, 30), which is no easy matter. As Levertov suggests in her title poem, offering a metaphor for the creative experience, "The stairway is not / a thing of gleaming strands." Rather, "It is of stone"—"A stairway of sharp / angles, solidly built"

> and a man climbing
> must scrape his knees, and bring
> the grip of his hands into play. (37)

Yet as the reader has seen in this far-ranging collection, "The cut stone / consoles his groping feet." Carefully wrought, celebrating man's potential but openly facing and exploring the sometimes unpleasant nature of the human animal and the world he has made for himself, "The poem ascends" (37).

DISCOVERIES AND EXPLORATIONS

Commenting on Levertov's work in his study of
American Poetry in the Twentieth Century, Kenneth Rexroth observed that "Denise Levertov writes at ease as a
woman about love, marriage, motherhood. . . . [H]er
poetry . . . is a poetry of sexual liberation of a human
person moving freely in the world."[5] But it is a hard-
earned "ease," not completely apparent until the 1964
volume *O Taste and See,* which follows *The Jacob's Ladder*
and which brings Levertov's personal explorations and
growing social concerns to bear on the subject of what it
means to live in the world as a woman. She writes of
sex and sexual politics with a directness and openness
of personal experience and public perspective that suggests she is redefining her sense of what she and other
women may expect as self-aware women.

When Levertov wrote early of marriage in *Here and
Now,* it was to affirm that women give up their identity
for the new relationship. "You have my / attention," a
wife declares to her husband, "And I have / your con-
stancy to / something beyond myself." She acknowledges that "The force / of your commitment charges
us—we live / in the sweep of it" ("The Marriage," *Earlier
Poems* 47). The husband is a creator, godlike, the wife
simply thrives in his presence. "It is you who make / a
world to speak of," she exclaims. "In your warmth the /
fruits ripen" (48):

> . . . If you listen
> it rains for them, then
> they drink. If you
> speak in response

> the seeds
> jump into the ground.
> Speak or be silent: your silence
> will speak to me (48).

Levertov knew that two ideas of woman contend in the whole being:

> The earthwoman by her oven
> tends her cakes of good grain.
> . . . .
> but the waterwoman
> goes dancing in the misty lit-up town
> in dragonfly dresses and blue shoes.
> ("The Earthwoman and the Waterwoman,"
> *Earlier Poems* 31–32)

Yet in *With Eyes at the Backs of Our Heads*, when "The Wife" speaks, it is simply to inform the listener that

> I give up on
> trying to answer my question,
> Do I love you enough?
>
> It's enough to be
> so much here (48).

How different the voice is that tells the reader "About Marriage" in *O Taste and See*, proclaiming "Don't lock me in wedlock, I want / marriage, an / encounter" (*Taste* 68). No longer simply nurtured in the radiance of the man's presence, the woman as wife speaks to a man as a sharing partner, confident of her individuality and demanding it.

DISCOVERIES AND EXPLORATIONS

The relationship of partners generates moments of intense physical and emotional connection which are recorded confidently and sensually by the poet:

> slowly
> smoothing in long
> > > sliding strokes
> our soapy hands along each other's
> slippery cool bodies
> ....
> our hands were
> flames
> stealing upon quickened flesh until
>
> no part of us but was
> sleek and
> on fire.
>
> > ("Eros at Temple Stream," *Taste* 55)

Of course there are times, too, of less radiantly positive connection. The reader realizes it in the ambiguous account of "Losing Track" in a relationship. Here the woman speaker likens herself to "a pier / half-in half-out of the water" whose lover swings toward and away from her, now nudging her awake "the way / a boat adrift nudges the pier," now swinging away before she knows she is "alone again long since." The final image of the woman as steady pier, "mud sucking at gray and black / timbers of me, / a light growth of green dreams drying," is a long way from Levertov's earlier accounts of passive acceptance in a relationship. The dissatisfaction now is obvious, though not, it seems, irrevocable.

For there has been "the pleasure of . . . communion" (*Taste* 74); and separateness, too, is part of relationship.

Without either romanticizing or lamenting, the poet acknowledges "The Ache of Marriage," the pain and promise of relationship: "thigh and tongue, beloved, / are heavy with it, / it throbs in the teeth." "We look," she explains, "for communion / and are turned away, beloved, / each and each." It can be a trap of biblical proportions:

> It is leviathan and we
> in its belly
> looking for joy, some joy
> not to be known outside it. . . .
>
> (*Taste* 5)

But, too, like the biblical ark, it signals hope and perhaps salvation in the eye of a storm for those who are, after all, "two by two in the ark of / the ache of it" (5).

The strongest evaluation in *O Taste and See* of the condition of women is not a personal portrait of an active relationship, but a chiding and inspiriting address to "Hypocrite Women." Immediately identifying her audience while grouping herself with them, the poet begins with an emphatic declaration of disappointment, anger, and dismay: "Hypocrite women, how seldom we speak / of our own doubts, while dubiously / we mother man in his doubt!" (*Taste* 70). In fact, the poet suggests, women seldom speak at all when they most need to, in response to masculine presumptions or insults, or simply for self-expression. Rather, they assume roles which, confirming male power and fantasies, make open communication impossible and corrupt or destroy their own promise.

"When a / dark humming fills us, a / coldness towards life," Levertov writes with understanding and anger on behalf of those who cannot or will not speak, "we are too much women to / own to such unwomanliness." Instead of honestly communicating their dissatisfactions with themselves and others, they assume a self-degrading image that men will accept and respond to: "Whorishly with the psychopomp / we play and plead—and say / nothing of this later." Levertov suggests that as inner vision is canceled by outer posturing, dreams are blighted. Ironically adopting and distorting advertising images, she explains:

> And our dreams,
> with what frivolity we have pared them
> like toenails, clipped them like ends of
> split hair.

> (*Taste* 70)

Lacking a language for self, women inherit male words in a man's world. Deliberately and crudely using "cunt," one of the ugliest reductive terms of dismissal or insult, Levertov makes her readers aware of language that reflects attitudes born of arrogance, while suggesting that it need not be so. Meaning is not inevitable in particular words, but measures usage and associations. It is possible to redefine even the most distorting and charged words, rethinking the selves they represent: "And if / . . . / a white sweating bull of a poet told us / our cunts are ugly—why didn't we / admit we have thought so too?" There is no "shame," the poet insists, taking us from graffiti toward mythos, for "(They are not for the eye!) / No, they are dark and wrinkled and hairy, / caves of the Moon" (*Taste* 70).

Levertov notes early in *O Taste and See* that "September 1961" marks "the year the old ones, / the great old ones / leave us alone on the road" ("September 1961," *Taste* 9). With H. D., Pound, and Williams increasingly silent, another generation is left to "count the / words in [their] pockets" (10).[6] Still finding new words, refining and redefining old ones, Levertov reveals the ways that experience takes a "multitude of forms" ("The Novices," *Taste* 57). She celebrates the physicality of "Our Bodies" (72), and reveals the stresses and rewards of ordinary moments of family relationships and relationship with the natural world ("Say the Word" 41–48). Too, she offers glimpses of extraordinary moments in myth ("Song for Ishtar" 3) and in dreams ("The Novices" 56–57), where "Knowing there [is] mystery" readers find themselves with the poet "listening / to the hum of the world's wood" (57).

In 1964 Levertov's "pockets" are full, the road she walks clear. *O Taste and See* consolidates and extends the strengths, subjects, and techniques of her earlier work. With *The Sorrow Dance* (1966) two years later, Levertov steps clearly into the new territory she will occupy for the next two decades, even as she continues to clarify

DISCOVERIES AND EXPLORATIONS

and enrich her own familiar ground. She not only offers "Perspectives" (*Sorrow* 65) on life lived day to day, on remembrances that have personal and public meaning, on what it means to be a poet and a woman, but she presents harrowing portraits of "Life at War" (79) in our time.

In her exploration of the relationships of the self to history and to the immediate moment, Levertov's narratives and myths continue to break free of culturally imposed and self-determined censorships, thereby deepening the spirit and defining more fully the human potential for action and reaction. Her emerging commitment to political and public poetry is a direct call to action, charting for her readers the stress lines of society as it begins to realize the enormous consequences of the Vietnam conflict. Her social awareness intensifying, Levertov accepts unequivocally that in both the personal and public spheres the writer is responsible for her words and must *"acknowledge their potential influence on the lives of others"* (*Poet* 114).

That the roots of responsibility to community run deep in the poet's personal experience, entwining private and public feelings, is evident in the moving "Olga Poems" (*Sorrow* 53–60) that Levertov writes in memorial to her much older sister Olga Levertoff, who died at the age of fifty. Recalling the childhoods they spent together but never quite shared because of differences in age and temperament, the poet recreates and speculates upon the impulses, desires, anxieties, and beliefs of the complex person "who now these two months long / is

bones and tatters of flesh in earth." What "the little sister" (53) rejected or was intuitively moved by, but
couldn't possibly understand, the adult poet now
knows and recognizes as an important seedbed of her
own understanding. Levertov remembers the ways
Olga "muttered into my childhood," sounding her
"rage / and human shame" (54) before poverty, her insistence on the worth of change, her love of the musical
words of hymns. She recognizes, too, what may be
some of the cost of such sensitivity, energy and commitment: "the years of humiliation, / of paranoia . . . and
near-starvation, losing / the love of those you loved."
Levertov ponders and pays homage to "compassion's
candle alight" nonetheless in her sister (60).

The sequence begins vividly with a sensory re-
creation of a child's vision, suggesting in its intensity
how important the older sister was to the younger, and
yet how separate and impenetrable she was. The reader
can virtually feel the heat "By the gas-fire" as Olga
kneels "to undress"

> scorching luxuriously, raking
> her nails over olive sides, the red
> waistband ring—
>
> . . . .
> Sixteen. Her breasts
> round, round, and
> dark-nippled . . . (*Sorrow* 53).

The reader recognizes, too, how absorbed and apart the
poet-child is, taking it all in for a lifetime's reference:

DISCOVERIES AND EXPLORATIONS

> (And the little sister
> beady-eyed in the bed—
> or drowsy, was I? My head
> a camera—) . . . (53).

But the adult poet is less concerned here with the physical moment than with comprehending the emotional tension and energy that shaped her sister and thereby affected her own life. Quickly attention shifts from a camera view of frozen time to moments of meditation and speculation, as Levertov, blending the child's point of view and the remembering adult's more reasoned understanding, relates the physical to the emotional.

Signs of stress predominate in the portrait of a young woman who seems at once forbiddingly old and vulnerably adolescent. They appear in "The high pitch of / nagging insistence" of Olga's voice; in the "lines / creased into raised brows"; and in "the skin around the nails / nibbled sore" (*Sorrow* 53). The teenager who "wanted / to shout the world to its senses," who knew from the age of nine what defined a "*slum*," was teased by her small sister reaching the same age, "admiring / architectural probity, circa / eighteen-fifty." But the poet, grown up and mixing memory with her own clear and strong adult social conscience, recognizes that in her dark browed and mercurial sibling was a purity of caring difficult to live with, but crucially valuable in its steady brightness: "Black one, black one, / there was a white / candle in your heart" (*Sorrow* 54).

Pondering the steps and missteps of Olga's life in relation to her own values and choices, Levertov conjures a vision of her sister's restlessness turned fearfully against itself. Half remembering and half creating moments of the past, Levertov recalls Olga's conviction that "everything flows" (*Sorrow* 55), expressed as nervous mutterings while she was "pacing the trampled grass" (54) of childhood playgrounds. These were words, the poet acknowledges, that "felt . . . alien" to the much quieter small child "look[ing] up from [her] Littlest Bear's cane armchair." Yet they were a source of comfort and bonding as well:

> . . . linked to words we loved
>
> from the hymnbook—*Time*
> *like an ever-rolling stream / bears all its sons away*—(55)

"But dread / was in her" sister, Levertov concludes, "a bloodbeat" of fear; and "against the rolling dark / oncoming river she raised bulwarks, setting herself / . . . / to change the course of the river." Recognizing clearly now the "rage for order" that "disordered her [sister's] pilgrimage" (55), Levertov's poem in a sense makes some order out of Olga's anguished life and partly clarifies her own as well:

> I had lost
>
> all sense, almost, of
> who she was, what—inside of her skin,
> under her black hair
> dyed blonde—
>
> it might feel like to be, in the wax and wane of the moon,

DISCOVERIES AND EXPLORATIONS

in the life I feel as unfolding, not flowing, the pilgrim
years—(56)

The poet pictures various scenes of Olga's immense fretful energy, and envisions the final "burned out" hospital days and nights: "while pain and drugs / quarreled like sisters in you" (*Sorrow* 57). She comes, after all, not to answers, but to questions which, being raised relentlessly, offer a recognition of the shapes of two lives linked in their diverse ways by questing and caring. As Levertov explains, addressing her sister, "I cross / so many brooks in the world, there is so much light / dancing on so many stones, so many questions my eyes / smart to ask of your eyes." Sounding the most crucial of them, she exclaims that "I think of your eyes in that photo, six years before I was born," remembering "the fear in them," wondering what became of the fear later, and "what kept / compassion's candle alight in you" through many difficult years (60).

The question of how to keep compassion's candle alight in the face of numbing horror and frustration is not simply one of hindsight or family discovery. It is one of the most perplexing questions that faced Levertov in the coming years, as her commitments were fired and tried by her growing awareness of what one nation can justify doing to another in the name of abstract words and public postures. To an extent, she found her answer in her early political poetry by looking to her own strengths as a poet and affirming the human capacity for creative imagining and communication. These were qualities to both counterbalance and reveal the powerful capacities of humankind for manipulations and destruction.

In "Life at War," the final grouping of her poems in *The Sorrow Dance,* Levertov presents a profoundly disturbing vision of violence that brings together unflinching directness of imagery with what seems in the context to be restrained, at times almost delicate, abstract language. The matter-of-fact picture of slaughter and mutilation is shocking, as is the contrast between presentation and meaning. But the very mix of gritty detail and controlled, often elegant, diction permits unusual recognitions. Levertov offers a language that confronts terrible human acts honestly, while still demonstrating the human potential for grace and imaginative reclamation. While indicting humankind for its savagery, she reminds herself and her readers, with irony but also with hopefulness, that human beings possess qualities of responsiveness that make a promise of peace thinkable.

"Man," Levertov explains, speaking with an almost metaphysical diction, is an animal "whose flesh / responds to a caress, whose eyes / are flowers that perceive the stars" and "whose understanding manifests designs / fairer than the spider's most intricate web" ("Life at War," *Sorrow* 79). But metaphysics disconcertingly collides with the immediate as the poet continues, suggesting with language that mixes abstractions and direct images, that this same human animal

still turns without surprise, with mere regret
to the scheduled breaking open of breasts whose milk
runs out over the entrails of still-alive babies,
transformation of witnessing eyes to pulp-fragments,
implosion of skinned penises into carcass-gulleys (80).

Levertov affirms that writer and readers alike are "the humans, men who can make; / whose language imagines *mercy, lovingkindness*," and have "believed one another / mirrored forms of a God we felt as good." But she suggests we must not refuse recognition that it is we "who do these acts, who convince ourselves / it is necessary," and that "these acts are done / to our own flesh; burned human flesh" (*Sorrow* 80). We must not use our ability with words to transform the truths of our deeds. Yet, too, because we *are* "men who can make," who can imagine a "God" that is "good," and a language that "imagines . . . / *lovingkindness*," our acts are recoverable.

"Knowledge" of hideous crimes of war, Levertov writes, "jostles for space / in our bodies along with all we / go on knowing of joy, of love":

our nerve filaments twitch with its presence
day and night,
nothing we say has not the husky phlegm of it in the saying,
nothing we do has the quickness, the sureness,
the deep intelligence living at peace would have.

(Sorrow 80)

Even as readers are compelled to know their guilt of action or of complacency, the poet has succeeded in reminding them with *her* visible joy of making, her love of language and clarity of vision, that they have the capacity for creation and for creative perception. Her readers have seen the ugliness of human affairs, but the surprising and disarming mix of formal beauty, strength and elegance of language, and horrific images, has made it possible for them to grasp the horror not just turn away in fear and loathing. Levertov, distancing herself from the nightmare even as she has looked into the heart of it, has offered readers a compassion that has made possible their seeing. She has begun to point toward a way of comprehending the violence of war that modern men "have breathed the grits of . . . all [their] lives, / the mucous membrane of [their] dreams / coated with it, the imagination / filmed over with the gray filth of it" (*Sorrow* 79).

In poems that are at times openly didactic yet lyrical, invariably questioning, *The Sorrow Dance* reveals the nature of human brutalities enacted on behalf of the political state, imagining the thoughts and lives of victims and victimizers alike ("What Were They Like," "The Altars in the Street," "Didactic Poem"). For all its shock, the impact is oddly that of relief, for at last the unspeakable is given voice. As Levertov suggests, "To speak of sorrow / works upon it"

> moves it from its
> crouched place barring
> the way to and from the soul's hall. . . .
>
> ("To Speak," *Sorrow* 63)

The reader discovers, too, that the dance of sorrow does not dispel the dance of joy. Thus the poems of *The Sorrow Dance* offer a "Hymn to Eros" (21), and a loving celebration of a son who "Moves among us from room to room of our life" (18). Levertov takes a cue from Thoreau, who suggests that "You must love the crust of the earth on which you dwell. You must be able to extract nutriment out of a sandheap. You must have so good an appetite as this, else you will live in vain" (quoted in "Joy," *Sorrow* 33).

Though the verses of *The Sorrow Dance* accept no denials of the human predicament, neither do they accept the easy answers of self-pity, cynicism, or despair. Throughout, Levertov is "faithful to / ebb and flow," affirming that: "There is no savor / more sweet, more salt / than to be glad to be / . . . myself" ("Stepping Westward," *Sorrow* 15). "If I bear burdens," she explains,

> they begin to be remembered
> as gifts, goods, a basket
>
> of bread that hurts
> my shoulders but closes me
>
> in fragrance. (16)

Whether exploring family memories, personal relationships, or public events in this, her most politically engaged book to date, Levertov brings her readers

to a recognition of their deep human flaws and
possibilities:

> The honey of man is
> the task we're set to: to be
> 'more ourselves'
> in the making:
>
> . . . .
> In our gathering, in our containing, in our
> working, active within ourselves,
> slowly the pale
> dew-beads of light
> lapped up from flowers
> can thicken,
> darken to gold:
>
> honey of the human.
> ("Second Didactic Poem," *Sorrow* 82–83)

Notes

1. Edward Dahlberg is being quoted by Charles Olson in Olson's
"Projective Verse" essay. Levertov cites the passage in *The Poet in the
World*, 13.

2. The discussion of "A Solitude" incorporates parts of my article "Exploring the Human Community: The Poetry of Denise Levertov and Muriel Rukeyser," *Sagetrieb* 3 (Winter 1984): 51–61.

3. Muriel Rukeyser, *The Life of Poetry* (New York: William Morrow, 1974) 40.

4. As Hannah Arendt explains it, "the so-called *Kristallnacht* or
Night of Broken Glass" was a night "when seventy-five hundred Jew-

DISCOVERIES AND EXPLORATIONS

ish shop windows were broken, all synagogues went up in flames, and twenty thousand Jewish men were taken off to concentration camps." See Hannah Arendt, *Eichmann in Jerusalem*, rev. and enl. ed. (New York: Viking, 1964) 39. See, too, Gideon Hausner, *Justice in Jerusalem* (New York: Harper, 1966) 42–43, for moving eye-witness accounts of the events of that night.

5. Kenneth Rexroth, *American Poetry in the Twentieth Century* (New York: Herder, 1971) 163.

6. On June 6, 1961, H. D. suffered a stroke and had great difficulty communicating. She died on Sept. 28, 1961. Williams had a cerebral hemorrhage on June 2, 1961 which made reading and writing extremely difficult for him. Pound also was ill in 1961 and was moving toward silence. See James Robinson, *H. D.: The Life and Work of an American Poet* (Boston: Houghton Mifflin, 1982) 433–34; Paul Mariani, *William Carlos Williams: A New World Naked* (New York: McGraw-Hill, 1981) 762–65; Noel Stock, *The Life of Ezra Pound* (New York: Pantheon, 1970) 455–59.

CHAPTER FOUR

The Poet in the World, Private Vision and Public Voice: *Relearning the Alphabet, To Stay Alive, Footprints, The Freeing of the Dust*

By the fall of 1967, with the United States "bitterly, bitterly at war" ("Tenebrae," *Relearning* 13) that "drags on, always worse" while "the soul dwindles sometimes to an ant / rapid upon a cracked surface" ("An Interim," *Relearning* 21), Levertov, like many American poets, found herself of necessity "writing more and more poems of grief, of rage, concerning . . . the . . . destruction of all that we feel passionate love for . . . by the mass murder we call war" (*Poet* 123). Recognizing the inevitable risk of losing veracity in polemic when mingling expressive language and rhetoric, Levertov in *Relearning the Alphabet* (1970), *To Stay Alive* (1971), *Footprints* (1972), and *The Freeing of the Dust* (1975)

THE POET IN THE WORLD

sought a poetry that might "have an effect upon the course of events by awakening pity, terror, compassion" without making it impossible to see the self or the world clearly or honestly. As she stated in 1975:

What those of us whose lives are permeated by a sense of unremitting political emergency, and who are at the same time writers of poetry, most desire in our work . . . is to attain to . . . osmosis of the personal and the public, of assertion and of song. . . . The didactic would be lyrical, the lyrical would be didactic. That is, at any rate, my own probably unattainable goal . . . (*Light* 128).

In the best of the poems published between 1970 and 1975, Levertov, deep in the darkest moments of her pilgrimage of discovery, shows the reader that:

political verses attain to . . . the condition of poetry . . . by the same means as any other kind: good faith, passionate conviction and, in equal measure, the precise operations of the creative imagination which sifts and sorts, leaps and pounces upon, strokes and shoves into a design the adored *words* that are the treasure of a faculty in love with its medium, even upon what [Turkish poet Nazim] Hikmet called the very "edge of darkness" (*Light* 129).

In fact, Levertov was "Relearning the Alphabet" in a gathering of moving elegies ("Tenebrae," "At David's Grave," "Despair"), recollections of travels in Vietnam ("In Thai Binh [Peace] Province," "Fragrance of Life, Odor of Death"), and experimental assemblages ("From a Notebook") that interlaced private and public history in snatches of newspaper headlines, bits of conversations overheard, letters read, political actions glimpsed and taken. She learned, too, a new coherence to her life's work, not simply making new lines into new poems, but recognizing links in already recorded experiences of family, womanhood, and politics. Levertov grouped old poems into new constructions that both clarified and redefined what had been the poet's experience of self and the world for much of a decade.

Never completely safe from the hazard of permitting the authority of a public poem to lie in the emotive power of the subject itself, Levertov succeeded more than most in heeding the warning of William Carlos Williams who had written that "the altered structure of the inevitable revolution must be *in* the poem, in it. Made of it. It must shine in the structural body of it. . . . Then . . . propaganda can be thoroughly welcomed . . . for by that it has been transmuted into the materials of art" ("Against the Weather," in *Light* 127). Refusing what Rilke called the "unlived life, of which one can die" (98), by 1975 Levertov was affirming the central place of "The Poet in the World" (*Poet* 107), even though a wary American audience was convinced by the prominence of confessional poetry to regard "the poem as always a private expression of emotion which

the reader is permitted to overhear" (*Light* 128). For as
Pablo Neruda had said, "Political poetry is more deeply
emotional than any other except love poetry. . . . You
must have traversed the whole of poetry before you become a political poet" (in *Light* 131).

Denying neither public nor private awareness, accepting that the ways into self and the ways toward others are inseparable, Levertov reminds her readers with
Rilke that "verses are not, as people imagine, simply
feelings . . . they are experiences" (in *Poet* 109):

In order to write a single poem, one must see many
cities, and people, and things; one must get to know
animals and the flight of birds, and the gestures that
flowers make when they open to the morning. One
must be able to return to roads in unknown regions,
to unexpected encounters, to partings long foreseen;
to days of childhood that are still unexplained. . . .
There must be memories of many nights of love, each
one unlike the others, of the screams of women in
labor. . . . But one must also have been beside the
dying, must have sat beside the dead in a room with
open windows and with fitful noises. And still it is
not yet enough, to have memories. One must be able
to forget them when they are many and one must
have the immense patience to wait till they are come
again. . . . Not till they have turned to blood within
us, to glance and gesture, nameless and no longer to
be distinguished from ourselves—not till then can it
happen that . . . the first word of a poem arises in
their midst and goes forth from them (*The Notebooks of
Malte Laurids Brigge*, in *Poet* 109–10).

The risks of opening oneself to experiences that are not within one's personal control are clearly measured throughout *Relearning the Alphabet*. But the rewards are also visible. Levertov notes the threat to poetic perception when the writer is confronted by history's numbing nightmares, and records the struggle back to confidence in the poet's purpose and capacities.

Pondering whether there is "anything / I write any more that is not / elegy" ("Notebook," *Relearning* 96), Levertov offers in the book's first section a gathering of laments for lost lives, diminished creative powers, skewed public sanity, and the erosion of human decency. She fears that her "strong sight, / . . . clear caressive sight . . . poet's sight I was given / that it might stir me to song, / is blurred":

> Because in Vietnam the vision of a Burning Babe
> is multiplied, multiplied,
> the flesh on fire
> . . . .
> infant after infant, their names forgotten,
> their sex unknown in the ashes,
> set alight, flaming but not vanishing.
> ("Advent 1966," *Relearning* 4)

In what seems a grotesque irony, the poet, an imaginative shaper and shifter of shapes who has the capacity to transform and reveal worlds, discovers herself transformed, as if caught in a dark fairy tale: "a monstrous insect / has entered my head, and looks out /

from my sockets with multiple vision." Yet this is not a
fantasy, but a reality that must not be taken as fiction:

> And this insect (who is not there—
> it is my own eyes do my seeing, the insect
> is not there, what I see is there)
> will not permit me to look elsewhere,
>
> or if I look, to see except dulled and unfocused,
> the delicate, firm, whole flesh of the still unburned.
> ("Advent 1966," *Relearning* 4)

Refusing to lie to herself or to others as she applies
her expressive language nakedly to the degradations of
current history, Levertov presents not the "deathsongs"
("The Cold Spring," *Relearning* 8) she fears have come to
dominate her verse, but songs of sorrow that carry hope
for life in their very capacity for directness and openness. The poet offers a revelation of, and contrast to, the
doublespeak that seems to dominate communication
at all levels. It has corrupted the conversations of
children:

> A five-year-old boy addresses
> a four-year-old. "When I say,
> *Do you want some gum?* say *yes.*"
> . . . .
> "Yes!" "Well yes means no,
> so you can't have any."
> ("An Interim," *Relearning* 21)

And it perverts the rhetoric of nations: " 'It became
necessary / to destroy the town to save it,' / a United

States major said today." If, as Levertov acknowledges, "language, virtue / of man, touchstone," is being "worn down by . . . / gross friction" (21) and "eroded as war erodes us" (22), it falls to the poet, as preserver and inventor, to teach her readers its sounds and meanings anew.

At best, the poet faces reluctant pupils, not willfully resistant, but almost innocent in their indifference: "And the buying and selling / buzzes at our heads, a swarm / of busy flies, a kind of innocence." Now, in the "*Fall of 1967*," appearances are taken for substance. At weddings "held in full solemnity" there is no "desire," but only "etiquette": "the nuptial pomp of starched lace; / a grim innocence." And while the poet hears "harsh rustlings / . . . / to remind [her] of shrapnel splinters" when she gets close to the "sharp-glinting" "Gowns of gold sequins" and "silver moiré" ("Tenebrae," *Relearning* 13) which are worn in pursuit of life's glitter, the scenes she presents here are not, by-and-large, grim, but are familiar domesticities with which readers can identify. The language is rich and evocative, the images often sentimental, even wistful; and to the extent that they find the scenes attractive, the poet implicates her readers in the indictment that finally undermines her portraits.

After picnics at the beach, when families head for home "burning with stored sun in the dusk," children, "sand in their hair, the sound of waves / quietly persistent at their ears," "fall asleep in the backs of a million station wagons." Neither they, nor their parents, who later "wake in the dark / and make plans" that "glitter

THE POET IN THE WORLD

into tomorrow" ("Tenebrae," *Relearning* 13), are attentive to murmurs of conscience, voices of reason and caring. Self-involved, satisfied, and neglectful, they are unable to recognize "at their ears the sound / of war. They are / not listening, not listening" (14). To make her readers listen to songs of responsibility, loss and anguish, in far away places like Vietnam and Biafra, and close to home in Detroit during the riots of 1967, Levertov explores new ways of arranging language and imagery. Juxtaposing a variety of writing styles and modes, she infuses her literal and figurative language with an energy and tension that comes from bringing together old and new communication patterns.

In "An Interim," her major experiment of the volume *Relearning the Alphabet*, Levertov assembles a verbal collage whose pieces combine to present a clear personal and public picture of the revolutionary times. Using news accounts of the arrest and trial of war resister de Courcy Squire for a kind of intermittent touchstone of courage and sacrifice throughout the poem, Levertov recounts in prose and verse her own coming to awareness as a war resister in the time before the trial of her husband Mitch Goodman, Dr. Benjamin Spock, and others. Too, she meditates on the nature of commitment and on resistence to government sanctioned violence.

Levertov begins in a general and impersonal way by recapitulating overheard casual conversation and by quoting from national news briefings and reports. She offers quick impressions of a society that is confused and manipulative at all levels, where in both ordinary talk and official government statements, illogic passes for logic. But she gradually personalizes the poem, placing her own experience at the center and thereby offering, not simply a critique of public policy and behavior, but also an understanding of history at the human level. Having gone "to the sea" with her husband before his trial for war resistance, "To repossess our souls" in the sun which is "warm bread, good to us, honest" (*Relearning* 22), the poet finds herself remembering another time, another seashore, where as a cranky child recovering from illness she was able to experience "Peace as grandeur. Energy / serene and noble." Bathed in the intimacy of the recollection, the reader recognizes with her "The quiet there is / in listening" to the "restlessness / of the sound of waves" which "transforms itself in its persistence / to that deep rest," and realizes with her that "Peace could be / that grandeur, that dwelling / in majestic presence, attuned / to the great pulse" (23). But the present steadily intrudes on both memory and quiet at the beach with news of war and protest.

Although momentarily at rest, "in the blue day, in the sweetness / of life . . . allowed / this interim before the trial" (*Relearning* 26), still the poet dreams of nightmare cities, "half Berlin, half Chicago—/ midwest German" where "many of us / [are] jailed":

> they led us through the streets,
> dressed in our prisoners' robes—
> smocks of brown holland—
> and the people watched us pass

THE POET IN THE WORLD

and waved to us, and gave us
serious smiles of hope (24).

She wakes to complex anger directed at supporters not
detractors, whose letters she quotes, thinking of "the
mild, / saddened people whose hearts ache / not for the
crimes of war, / . . . / but for us [poet and husband]."
Levertov mixes verse with prose, as if to ensure dealing
both expressively and directly with the "cramp of fury"
that forms against sincerely concerned but misguided
friends. As though to counterbalance and correct "The
sympathy of mild good folk" whose misplaced empa-
thy, though heartfelt, is "The white of egg without the
yolk, / it soothes their conscience and relieves / the irri-
tations of their doubt" (26), the poet sounds a litany of
political activists without offering much by way of detailed explanation.

The poem fills with names of people whose lives
and actions were part of the poet's experience of the
moment, but whom the reader may not know or recognize: Mitch, Bob Gilliam, Dennis Riordan, Norman
Morrison, Alice Hertz. Although it may frustrate a reader's desire to get the facts straight and might create
some resentment at being shown a private experience
but kept from full comprehension of it, the matter-of-
fact presentation of characters and events, offered without notes, is part of the poem's strategy.[1] For these are
not historical figures whose actions and contributions
should be summarized neatly for a reader's edification.
And Mitch Goodman's trial for conspiracy to oppose a

military draft, the details of which are not described, was not simply a textbook event to be outlined; it was an action lived. History, the poet seems to say, is, after all, people living their lives, knowable to a few, unknown and unknowable to many. Failure to see that all history is human history leads toward the sort of dehumanizing illogic that can destroy a village in order to save it.

Levertov believes that there are some whose courage offers comfort, and in whose words language "draws breath again," whose "*yes* and *no*" is a "true testimony of love and resistance" (*Relearning* 27). For the broad picture, against which readers can imagine and measure the other actions of war resistance upon which the poem focuses, Levertov offers news accounts of de Courcy Squire's protest, incarceration, and fast:

> . . . *arrested with 86 others Dec. 7. Her crime:*
> *sitting down in front of a police wagon*
> *momentarily preventing her friends from being*
> *hauled to prison. Municipal Judge Heitzler*
> *handed out 30-day suspended sentences to several others*
> *accused of the same offense, but condemned*
> *Miss Squire to 8 months in jail and fined her*
> *$650. She had said in court 'I don't think there should be*
> *roles like judge and defendant.'*
>
> . . . .
> *Denied visitors, even her parents;*
> *confined to a locked cell without running water*
> *or a toilet.*
>> *On January 29th, the 53rd day of her fast,*
>> *Miss Squire was removed to a hospital* (22, 26).

THE POET IN THE WORLD

For the most part, however, the poet presents not a picture of confidence, but of a struggle to sustain conviction while acknowledging confusion; and readers are asked to share it. Assembling the bleak fragments Levertov offers, they find they all need the example of "the few" whose response "Might burn through the veil that blinds / those who do not imagine the burned bodies / of other people's children" (27). Individuals may not be able to dispel the dark, but they can see it clearly:

> We need them.
> Brands that flare to show us
> the dark we are in,
> to keep us moving in it (28).

The knowledge gained from information presented and information withheld, from the poem's mixed modes and moods, from the variety of denotative and connotative observations, demands attention. And if readers are attentive they will have begun to know their living history. For Levertov, writing in a violent and troubled decade, this is the poet's gift.

Speaking in 1979 of a "writer's responsibility," Levertov observed that "the basic responsibility is that the writer should recognize he is a social being, that he really lives in a world with other people, and that his words and deeds may have some weight with others."[2] The conviction lies at the center of Levertov's social writing in *Relearning the Alphabet* and the books that follow. But even in poems that define a writer's responsibility, the poet's subject and language of expression need not always be explicitly political, as the reader sees in Levertov's poem in praise of the poet's music, "A Tree Telling of Orpheus" (*Relearning* 81). Placed near the end of the book that begins elegiacally and concludes hopefully, this evocative long poem serves to clarify the goals and accomplishment of many of the more political poems of *Relearning the Alphabet*. The poet is preparing her readers for "the ah! of praise" which she utters in almost the final lines of the book (120).

Levertov once observed of Robert Duncan that "we share a love of fairytales. He never separates the world of magic, or lore, from the grievous world of daily history. He is a mythologist."[3] In a similar way "A Tree Telling of Orpheus" is the work of a mythologist whose transformations illuminate the poet's place in the daily history of a difficult time.

Mythical consciousness, philosopher Ernst Cassirer wrote, "lives in the immediate impression, which it accepts without measuring it by something else."[4] "Differentiation and stratification," the stuff of science and social science, "is totally alien" to it, for the image it renders "is not through something else and does not depend on something else as its condition":

on the contrary it manifests and confirms itself by the . . . intensity of its presence, by the . . . force with which it impresses itself upon consciousness. Whereas scientific thought takes an attitude of inquiry and doubt toward the "object" with its claim to objectivity and necessity, myth knows no such opposition. It

THE POET IN THE WORLD

"has" the object only insofar as it is overpowered by it; it does not possess the object by progressively building it but is . . . possessed by it.[4]

Shaping a myth even as it seeks to describe the ways myths work, "A Tree Telling of Orpheus" brings Levertov's readers face to face with the power of the poet in the world.

Though, as the title suggests, the poem is a long narrative told in the first person by a participant in a special event, there is no relationship established at the outset between an "I" and the world. Rather, the tale opens with sensory impressions, sentence fragments that are as much dislocations of expectation as they are locations in the world of the narrative. The first half-line reading simply "White dawn. Stillness" is followed on the page by white space the size of a full word. It seems to suggest a disembodied voice speaking, the words hanging in space; and though the impression of place is powerful, the place itself is unspecified. Immediately engaged by the vivid sensory quality of the description, the reader is loosened from familiar ground. And the contradictory first impression of spatial immediacy and disconnection continues. While a landscape is described—the place is a valley near a sea that has "treeless horizons" and is engulfed by "white fog"—the gathering description is full of confusing signals. Paradoxically, even as spatial and sensory boundaries between a "here" and a "beyond" are defined, the poem seems to collapse such distinctions. In a changeless valley, where new experience is only hinted at like the "sea-wind" bringing "rumors / of salt," a "rippling" begins and "[draws] nearer." Yet the reader cannot be sure of its source, or direction, or even if it is sound or simply motion. Like the "white fog" which "didn't stir," it surrounds him, seeming inexplicably both static and dynamic. It seems that this is the stirring of forest leaves before some unusual, magical, and still unrealized happening. As the narrator observes: "my own outermost branches began to tingle, almost as if / fire had been lit below them, too close, and their twig-tips / were drying and curling." But like the tale-telling tree, readers can only wait, discovering both their sensations and the limits of their vantage, inadequately informed, unable to make satisfactory logical connections, yet enriched by the happening and "deeply alert" (*Relearning* 81).

Immediate experience gives way to factual information as the teller seeks associations that will clarify events. The poem's title is the key that unlocks mysteries. When the speaking voice announces that "I was the first to see him, for I grew / out on the pasture slope, beyond the forest," the reader recognizes that "he" must be Orpheus, mythical singer, son of the muse Calliope. The narrator explains that:

> He carried a burden made of
> some cut branch bent while it was green,
> strands of a vine tight-stretched across it. From this,
> when he touched it, and from his voice
> which unlike the wind's voice had no need of our
> leaves and branches to complete its sound,
>
> came the ripple.
>
> (*Relearning* 81)

THE POET IN THE WORLD

Here the reader recognizes what the tree cannot: the
lyre which accompanies the wondrous tones. He recognizes, too, that the voice which speaks to him is making
a reasonable effort, even a scientific one, to comprehend through analogy the strange experience:

He was a man, it seemed: the two
moving stems, the short trunk, the two
arm-branches, flexible, each with five leafless
                                                twigs at their ends,
and the head that's crowned by brown or gold grass,
bearing a face not like the beaked face of a bird,
        more like a flower's (81).

But definition achieved by measuring experience in
relation to some other familiar object or context, is, after
all, inadequate. As the tree is roused into awareness of
itself and the world, Levertov envisions the poet's crucial "social function," "to awaken sleepers" (*Poet* 5). The
process reveals what Philip Wheelwright, writing in
general of the mythic consciousness, noted as "an inde-
finable . . . coalescence of things"[5]:

        I seemed to be singing as he sang, I seemed to know
        what the lark knows; all my sap
                was mounting towards the sun that by now
                        had risen, the mist was rising, the grass
        was drying, yet my roots felt music moisten them
        deep under earth.

Even further, the awakened tree discovers that "it was
no longer sounds only that made the music: / he spoke,
and as no tree listens I listened, and language / came
into my roots" (*Relearning* 82).

Levertov believes that poetry embodies the full consciousness of human knowledge, and that the poet's song of inner and outer worlds—"of the dreams of man, wars, passions, griefs"—shows men their fears, their energies, their potential for innate understandings, and for change. The discomforting but invigorating power of transformations is such that even a tree "understood words—ah, it seemed / my thick bark would split like a sapling's that / grew too fast in the spring" (*Relearning* 82). In the images of fiery destruction and growth, and in the repetitive, almost incantatory rhythms, the singer offers revelations of contradictions and continuities, beginnings linked to endings, the troubling but exciting discoveries of heightened consciousness:

> Fire he sang,
> that trees fear, and I, a tree, rejoiced in its flames.
> New buds broke forth from me though it was full summer.
> As though his lyre . . .
> were both frost and fire, its chords flamed
> up to the crown of me.
> I was seed again.
> I was fern in the swamp.
> I was coal (82–83).

Wrenched out of stasis by the music, "Clumsily, / stumbling over our own roots," the trees learned the joy of motion, the promise of possibility rather than restriction: "We learned to dance, / . . . / and words he said / taught us to leap and to wind in and out." Such recognition once achieved will never be lost. If the poet, having awakened his listeners, must eventually sing their "sun-

THE POET IN THE WORLD

dried roots back into earth," providing "all-night rain of music so quiet" (*Relearning* 84), and must face his own limits and fated death, the memory of his song remains. "It is said he made his earth-journey," the tree explains, "It is said they felled him":

Perhaps he will not return.

But what we have lived

comes back to us.

We see more.

We feel, as our rings increase,
something that lifts our branches, that stretches our furthest
leaf-tips

further.

The wind, the birds,

do not sound poorer but clearer,
recalling our agony, and the way we danced.
The music!

(*Relearning* 85)

In 1968 and 1969, when the choice often seemed to the poet to be "Revolution or death," Levertov, like her mythic singer, offered the music of "*Life that / wants to live*" ("Notebook," *Relearning* 92). The prose and verse fragments of personal and public history gathered in "From a Notebook: October '68–May '69" are an "act / of passionate attention" (98) to the possibilities of both new starts and continuations even as "The War / comes home to us" in "the clubs, the gas, / bayonets, bullets" (107) of Berkeley's People's Park, or in the violence in Mayor Daley's Chicago. Thinking through and personalizing the concept of revolution, Levertov brings the reader to a momentary vision of wholeness emerging from terrifying destruction. Still hearing the words of a song that blared in the background of a demonstration, proclaiming *"change is now / change is now / things that seem to be solid are not"* (108)[6], the poet presents her own affirmation: "Maybe what seems / evanescent is solid" (109). Revolution is not simply "the circular: an exchange / of position" (103), nor is it but a radical break with old habits or value systems. It is something organic, "pervasive" (102), realized in "a crown of tree" which "raises itself out of the heavy / flood." It is seen when "The floodwaters / stir, mud / swirls to the surface" (108):

> A hand, arm,
> lifts in the crawl—
> hands, arms, intricate
>   upflashing—
>   a sea full of swimmers!
>   their faces' quick steady
>   lift for air. . . . (109)

Change is not linear. "Time," as Levertov suggests, paraphrasing the old Canon in Denis Saurat's *Death and the Dreamer*, "is not a sequence, / as man's simplicity thinks, but radiates / out from a center." In "every direction" and "all / dimensions" it is "radiant" (105).

The vision is romantic, but has not been offered at the expense of engagement with the grim realities of the day. Having looked hard and angrily at the spasm of hate that shakes society, Levertov still affirms that "Love / aches me" (*Relearning* 93): love for community under threat, and love for language that is the poet's special burden and solace. "Without a terrain in which, to which, I belong," Levertov wrote in one of her notebook entries, "language itself is my one home, my Jerusalem" (97). Armed with a sense of place and with the energy of her commitments, Levertov insists by the end of *Relearning the Alphabet*, that with "Anguish, ardor" we can find "Joy—a beginning. . . . / To relearn the ah! of knowing" (110).

Writing recently for a symposium on religion and intellectual life, Levertov called attention to remarks by George MacDonald, who said that "When the desire after system or order degenerates from a need into a . . . ruling idea, it closes . . . like an unyielding skin over the mind." This, together with Martin Buber's observation that "To produce is to draw forth, to invent is to find, to shape is to discover," serves to define clearly both the thematic and formal concerns of Levertov's next work, *To Stay Alive*, published in 1971.[7] For here she finds new forms in old, shaping separate poems that had appeared elsewhere into a new configuration. The poet refuses the stifling or corrupting demands of predetermined systematization, whether personal, social, or aesthetic.

"As one goes on living and working," Levertov begins in the "Author's Preface" of *To Stay Alive*, "themes recur, transposed into another key perhaps. Single poems that seemed isolated perceptions when one wrote them prove to have struck the first note of a scale or a melody." The artist, then, is, "willy-nilly, weaving a fabric, building a whole in which each discrete work is a part that functions . . . in relation to all the others" (*Stay Alive* vii). In rethinking the relationship of early poems to late, Levertov clarifies not only poetic patterns, but personal ones as well. Juxtaposing the "Olga Poems" and verses from "Life at War" in *The Sorrow Dance*, with poems from "Elegies" and "From a Notebook: October '68—May '69" in *Relearning the Alphabet*, and new poems that report the "Daily Life" (79) of our time, Levertov records current affairs, affirms human rights, and explores the directions of her own life in relation to the world.

The poet acknowledges that

'There comes
             a time
                  when only anger
                             is love'—(81).[8]

But stirred, too, by a broader love that is part of routine life, "the love that streams / towards me daily, letters and poems, husband and child" (82), Levertov mingles rage, sorrow, and unquenchable hope. The regrouped poems, added to the new, move the reader from a portrait of the poet's lost sister "working / in her way for Revolution" (65) that is not political and governmental, but human and individual, to a picture of all "who believe / life is possible" (84) and were willing to breath the smoke and face the violence of Berkeley and Washington to confirm it. Through it all, the poet is historian, witness, participant.

THE POET IN THE WORLD

The long poem that is assembled as "Staying Alive" offers fragments shored against society's ruin, and the poet's. With "sharp stabs of recall" (*Stay Alive* 38), Levertov takes the reader on a journey through her remembered past toward a reconciliation with the present and a momentarily opened window onto the future. In the summer of 1970, returning to Europe after ten years and "to 'merry London' as to a nest" (65) after twenty years, the poet ponders whether such a personal journey undertaken while "Amerika / far away / tosses in fever" is merely an indulgence, a "cop-out" (60). Yet as she rediscovers "friends whose lives / have been knit with mine a quarter century" (66), and, quoting nineteenth-century English essayist Thomas De Quincey, envisions Olga and her youthful self beneath "The dreamy lamps / of stonyhearted Oxford Street" (64), the poet recognizes that she carries America with her: "violent Amerika," "of whose energy, / in whose fever, in whose wild / cacophonous music" she has "lived / and will live." Having returned to England only to discover just how far she has travelled psychologically, Levertov accepts that she had "left, unknowing," a "gentleness . . . kindness / of the *private life*." In America, she "gained instead the tragic, fearful / knowledge of *present history*, / of . . . 'life / ferocious and sinister.' " Yet, "life is in me," she proclaims:

> . . . a love for
> what happens, for
> the surfaces that are their own
> interior life . . . (66).

Though Levertov had written a month before in Boston that "At my unhappiest, / . . . I want / oblivion" (*Stay Alive* 63), she refuses it daily in her "hunger for revelation" through the senses:

> I don't want it for long.
>   I don't know
> how to be mute, or deaf, or blind,
> for long, but
> wake and plunge into next day
> talking . . .
> listening, even if what I'm hearing
> has the *approaching* sound of terror (64).

Rejecting system but not coherence, chaos but not energy, the poet, having gained distance and perspective, returns to America to discover not the "lava" of a volcanic social explosion she thinks she left, but a rhythm of daily life:

> a substance that expands and contracts, a rhythm
> different from the rhythm of history,
> though history is made of the same
> minutes and hours (75).

For good and ill, this is a world both old and new at once, filled with moments that are both familiar and disconcerting. Levertov experiences by turns the terror of "the swinging clubs of the cops" (*Stay Alive* 77), the happiness of "momentary community" amidst war-protesting friends, the anger and sadness of losing companions through suicide, the simple pleasures of place and possessions—"these small / objects of dailiness each with its history, / books, photos" (75). Amidst the comforts and discomforts of feeling both located and displaced, the poet centers herself, submitting emotionally and intellectually to the advice of a friend who suggested to another:

> imagine yourself
> quiet and intent sitting there,
> not running from blocked
> exit to blocked exit (71).

Acknowledging the shifting surfaces of her world, Levertov accepts, nonetheless, as a friend suggested, the recognition that "it's your well / go deep into it / into your own depth as into a poem" (*Stay Alive* 72). There she can uncover, as French novelist and philosopher Albert Camus, whom she quotes, discovered, "inside myself, even in the very midst of / winter, an invincible summer" (77). Conrad Aiken once asked, "Is not poetry an affirmation, even when it is fullest of despair?" As if in answer, *To Stay Alive* provides emphatically what Aiken called "that taproot sort of affirmation, a blood-filled affirmation deeply rooted in the world— we need it now more than ever."[9]

Even as Levertov was composing the long experiments in mixed modes of *Relearning the Alphabet* and *To Stay Alive,* she continued to write the brief lyric meditations that are gathered in her next book, *Footprints* (1972). These are predominantly illuminations of ordinary moments, reflections on subjects ranging from a sense of place and the routines of complex domesticities

("By Rail through the Earthly Paradise, Perhaps Bed-fordshire," "Brass Tacks," "A Defeat in the Green Mountains"), to the experience of "Living with a Paint-ing" or rediscovering the sense of sound amidst stran-gers and friends "At the 'Mass Ave Poetry Hawkers' Reading in the Red Book Cellar." Although there are occasional verses that focus directly upon the devastat-ing political situations of the time ("Overheard over S.E. Asia," "The Day the Audience Walked Out on Me, and Why"), and some that reveal more generally the poet's public anger ("The Sun Going Down upon Our Wrath"), typically these are poems which in their atten-tion to the everyday comprise companion pieces to the probing public explorations and self-examinations of *Re-learning the Alphabet* and *To Stay Alive.*

The lyrics in *The Freeing of the Dust* published three years later in 1975, however, represent an expansion of Levertov's range of experience and mark her deepest plunge into the depths of intertwined public and per-sonal anger, loss, and recovery. In 1972, just before Richard Nixon's reelection, she traveled to Hanoi, North Vietnam, together with her old friend and fellow poet Muriel Rukeyser, and war protester Jane Hart, wife of Michigan Senator Philip Hart. Sights at the Bach Mai Hospital in particular prompted the searing verses, ter-rifyingly and tenderly wrought, which are collected in an early section of the book. Describing the scene in an essay for *American Report,* February 26, 1973, Levertov observed that "one is never fully prepared for the sight of suffering" (*Poet* 134). Nonetheless, the reportorial prose, later collected in *The Poet in the World*, prepares her readers for the poems that will follow to lay bare the agony of war:

> We are stunned by the encounter with two patients' cases in particular. . . . These are two children, boys, each in small separate rooms, each with a silent, stony-faced mother sitting by his bedside.
>
> One has lost both legs from just below the knee. His left arm and his body are bandaged, too. He lies on his back, expressionless, toying and toying with a little spool of some kind he holds in his hands. . . .
>
> The other is a couple of years older. Bomb fragments have lodged in his brain, as well as elsewhere in his body. His head is swathed in bandages—his face looks out of its turban with a strange expression, disoriented. . . . We cannot speak. Going out into the sunlight again, we take photos of bomb craters in the gardens. (134)

When Levertov speaks in her poems, "try[ing] to bring / the war home," recounting and imagining what her "dry burning eyes" have seen "In Thai Binh (Peace) Province" (*Freeing* 35), the power of protest takes on new dimensions. These observations are not the promptings of principle only, nor indignant discourses spurred by the news of the day, nor even accusations delivered from the front lines of active war resistance in America. Rather, they are an eloquent eye-witness testimony of the human cost of war, revealing the authority of firsthand experience.

As if to ready and steady the reader, the poet moves him gradually toward direct contact with the waking nightmare in Vietnam. Foremost among the first impressions in *The Freeing of the Dust* is simply a generalized sense of hearing "A Sound of Fear," noticed in the reverberant "clop, clop, clop, every night" ("A Sound of Fear" 25) of a woman who descends and reascends the hollow stairs of a twelve-story building rather than ride the elevator for fear, perhaps, of violence, or of the enclosed space, or of having to meet someone. In a separate part of the small fortress, fighting isolation and dehumanization herself, cut off from clear sight but not from hearing or imaginative speculation, the poet's speaker seems to suggest that anxiety is now a pervasive state of being. It hangs in the air, thwarting community, unrelated to any specific cause that might be easily identified and managed.

Moving the reader closer to the heart of fear that still lies somewhere off in "The Distance," Levertov turns her attention from the symbolic urban American prison of the apartment complex, and the elevator compartment and stairway halls within it, to the very real "ugly but not uninhabitable cells" where war protestors are processed. And she compels the reader to imagine even further the "cruel [tiger] cages . . . built in America" for Vietnamese political prisoners. Her poems, though, finally seek to celebrate the human spirit under stress. For "over there" in Vietnam, the poet explains, "they mourn / the dead," yet "they too sing. / They too rejoice" (*Freeing* 27). But in the United States, with no convincing portrait of moments of affirmation available, only the image of suffering lingers.

When the poet is herself in Vietnam, confronted by "bombed village schools, the scattered / lemon-yellow cocoons at the bombed silk-factory," "yet another child with its feet blown off," she is able nonetheless to see at firsthand some splinter of "Peace within the / long war. / . . . life, unhurried, sure, persistent" ("In Thai Binh [Peace] Province," *Freeing* 35). While being there shocks the senses, deepens the rage, and burns images of loss into the poet's consciousness, immediacy also allows fuller vision of a sense of place, a view of the quiet moments that surround the horrific. Levertov can see what it means "To live / beyond survival," even amidst the devastations of war ("Dragon of Revolutionary Love" 41). With all her tears used up for the moment, she will use her clear sight:

> to photograph within me
> dark sails of the river boats,
> warm slant of afternoon light
> apricot on the brown, swift, wide river,
> village towers—church and pagoda—on the far shore,
> and a boy and small bird both
> perched, relaxed, on a quietly grazing
> buffalo (35).

As she explained in a second *American Report* essay published on March 12, 1973, "self-reproach can be a form of self-indulgence":

> In other words, the impetus to our own
> development toward the social change which alone
> can bring peace, can come more strongly from the
> knowledge of how humane, kindly . . . and
> constructive it is, after all, possible for human beings
> to be, than from grief, anger, and remorse when these
> emotions are separated from such positive knowledge.
> Courage is patient.
>
> (*Poet* 145)

As the poet's public understanding is tried, tem-
pered, and changed by her expanding outer experience,
so her rediscovery of herself is deepened by the intensity of immediate private experiences. Confronting her
own dissolving marriage in the early 1970s, a kind of
echo of the world at war, Levertov found amidst pain
and sadness the same spirit of renewal. Although more
private than any of the poet's work to date, her verses at
this time are not the self-indulgent revelations that
dominated the work of many 1960s poetic confessors.
Neither shrill, nor an invitation to psychoanalysis or
voyeurism, these dignified poems revealing the experience of living at "Crosspurposes" (*Freeing* 54), "Divorcing" (66), finally, of "Living Alone" (59), offer
narratives, parables, dreams, and meditations, that
show the reader not just the condition of one relationship, but reveal more broadly the limits and possibilities
of personal relationships under stress.

"Crosspurposes," the first of a group of poems ex-

THE POET IN THE WORLD

ploring a failed relationship, begins with melodramatic clangor: "With dread she heard the letter / fall into the drop." But in the tale that follows, the poet studiously avoids the sensationalism which the opening lines seem to invite. Still, there is no crossed purpose to Levertov's intention here. The poet, announcing a subject fraught with the potential for high drama and extreme emotion only to diffuse it, highlights the reader's awareness that her story is not a blow-by-blow account of the collapse of shared lives, but is rather a revelation of the complex ways individuals cope with irrevocable change. She writes of facing up to "Decision and fear" (*Freeing* 54), however painful it may be.

Almost immediately, Levertov sets an opposition between calm surface actions and turbulent inner thoughts. The dread of the dropped letter, still to be explained, is juxtaposed with a quiet portrait of a warm afternoon picnic among friends. While the day slowly gives way to evening, "the round charcoals" "incandescent" and flickering in the dying light of the "sun's fire," the speaker's mind darts and dives through the much darker terrain of anxiety and fears that define her worries about having mailed a "letter [that] was crawling / grayly north to pronounce sentence, / to send a lifetime out into exile" by declaring a marriage ended. The tension inherent in the apparent divergence of inner and outer worlds, however, gradually passes into the realization that the inner world of feeling and thought and the outer world of activity are twins. Even a simple frisbee game perceived by the mind's eye is as much a reflection of, and metaphor for, the hidden emotional life as it is an antidote to it. The poet observes that "nothing would show" her absorption in the unspoken drama of the shattering of a relationship:

> Even she herself
> could not have said for sure, as she played,
> the letter was moving north already
> to indict her history.

(*Freeing* 54)

But the peculiar flight of the frisbee, tossed from player to player, seems increasingly to be a correlative for the shared life that is coming apart:

> Magically the tangerine disc
> glides and curves and chooses
> to land in someone's outflung hand, sometimes
> even in unpracticed hers; gracious caprice.
> Or circles back to fingers that sent it forth.
> The game is a dance. (54)

The final steps of the dance of relationship, an exchange of "Two letters [which] passed each other, carried / north and south," suggest how disconnected the sad choreography has become. The wife's letter, just mailed, explains that "Our journey has come to a dead end / we mustn't cower by that wall, / skin our fingers trying to scale it" or "perish there":

> "now we must each take one of the narrow paths,
> . . . parallel
> to the wall at first,
> then bearing away from it,
>   wider and wider apart

> from it and from
> each other."

(Freeing 55)

The husband's letter, already received, declares in contrast, "We must return / to sunrise . . . to seeing / one / another / anew" (55). But for the speaker of the painful tale, it is a sunset truth, clear in the dying light. The rhythm, movement, music of relationship, are separate and will remain so:

> . . . two songs
> each in a different key,
> two fables told
> in different countries,
> two pairs of eyes looking past each other
> to different distances. (56)

"Living Alone" (*Freeing* 59), suddenly freed from the habits that gradually dull the capacity to perceive the sights and sounds of one's environment, the poet begins to learn anew the shape of the spaces and places she inhabits. She recognizes, too, that her map is as much emotional as physical, a terrain drawn in childhood that continues to impinge upon and partially define the adult's world. Interrupting long descriptive lines with fragments of memory, meditation, and perception to suggest the halting perceptual process by which definitions of landscape and mindscape are interwoven, the poet declares:

And if I coast, down toward home, spring evenings, silently,
a kind of song rising in me to encompass

Davis Square and the all-night
cafeteria and the pool hall,
it is childhood's song, surely no note is changed,
sung in Valentines Park or on steep streets in the map of my
    mind
in the hush of suppertime, everyone gone indoors.
Solitude within multitude seduced me early.

("Living Alone [I]," *Freeing* 59)

Yet sight is as clouded as it is clarified by the necessities of facing the world alone. The effort to see clearly through the hurt of isolation and separation becomes a struggle that defines both self and place. "Some days," the speaker exclaims, "living alone, / there's only knowledge of silence" ("Living Alone [II]," *Freeing* 60). At the end of the relationship, the speaker discovers she has "entered sadness / as one enters a mountain cloud" and that "cloudy sadness, vague arms around us, / carries us like a bundle" ("Cloud Poems" 62) blurring her vision. Though unafraid of her solitude, she finds herself scarred by disabling fears of both loss and healing:

> Our blood's not sure
>   if it can circulate,
> now we are cut apart.

("Divorcing" 66)

> . . . is the wound
> my life has suffered
>
>   healing too fast,
> shutting in bad blood?

("Strange Song" 67)

And waking nightmares of grief distort what is "visible / to mind's eye" as the speaker envisions herself helpless, "hoisted off the / earth of my energies like / a bug overturned" ("Grief" 68).

But after all, the ending is seen clearly as a beginning rather than a completion, frightening but exciting with promise. Coming together for a final ritual of separation, the two people on the brink of parting "After half a lifetime," having rediscovered the capacity to see again with their own eyes and sensibilities, offer a "Libation." They wish for each other "happiness," meaning "growth, branching, / . . . yielding blossoms and fruit and the sharp odor of dreams" (*Freeing* 69).

The final optimistic lines of "Libation," the last poem of the sequence, offer a fitting conclusion to the marriage group. Though seemingly simple, they compel the reader into active participation as a percipient maker of meaning, just as the poet has drawn meaning out of, and placed meaning into, the surfaces of her life. Apparently straightforward, the lines are enriched by the poet's spare language, arrangement of line-break, and the absence of punctuation save for the final period: "After these months of pain we begin / to admit our new lives have begun" (*Freeing* 69).

Because the eye runs forward while the mind moves more haltingly, hesitating over various syntactic possibilities before assembling the whole, the simple declarative lines gain a multiplicity of meanings. Each supports the others as the reader assembles the thought in a variety of possible ways. Thus an initial response, the generalized "After these months . . . we begin" (the reader stops here at least briefly at the white space at the end of the line) slides momentarily into the still generalized, but more specific, "After these months . . . we begin / to admit." At this point the admission seems to be of emotions and thoughts that were difficult to acknowledge or express. The next phrase, "our new lives have begun," is momentarily perceived as a distinct thought, separate and whole in its syntactic completeness. This quickly becomes what the syntax finally leads to: "After these months of pain we begin / to admit our new lives have begun." Had the poet placed a comma or her linebreak after "pain," thereby positioning "begin" and "to admit" in the closer proximity that syntax seems to demand ("After these months of pain, we begin / to admit" or "After these months of pain / we begin to admit"), or had she actually added the word "that" after "admit" where it is only implied now ("to admit that our new lives have begun"), the lines would have been more explicit, but less meaningful. And perhaps as the separating couple manages a "smile" of recognition and pleasure that they have achieved a momentary but real victory over the adversities that beset them for so long, the reader smiles too, both with relief at the optimism (accented by the amusing thump of "begin / begun"), and with pleasure at the recognition of a poet careful of craft even at moments of deepest feeling (*Freeing* 69).

Having explored in *The Freeing of the Dust* the need to look outward to the world to know another, and inward to comprehend and accept the self, Levertov seems to sum up the nature of the experience in recounting a "Conversation in Moscow" (*Freeing* 85). The longest poem in the book, public but not topically political in the manner of the Vietnam antiwar poems, private without being intimate like the divorce poems, "Conversation" offers a dialogue between the individual's consciousness and the community's, between disciplines, and between cultures, revealing in the process the complex relationship of language to thought and feeling.

The scene unfolds itself slowly and comfortably, as a Russian biologist, poet, and historian, fellow "members of the tribe of the word," talk animatedly after dinner with the visiting American writer. Lacking a common tongue to share thoughts and feelings, all must entrust themselves to "the woman who is / our interpreter." For each, foreign yet familiar in their shared creative terrain, it is an act not only of cautious necessity, but of faith in communication. For the interpreter herself, it is an almost impossible demand, for "She knows she must *be* / each of us turn by turn and / each at once" (*Freeing* 85). As both the most separate and the most dependent, the American poet not only discovers the crucial problem of language that isolates individuals and nationalities, but realizes, too, that community is more than a matter of words. Relying heavily on her "sister" interpreter, almost as a blind woman might rely on the sighted, Levertov comes to recognize that all the senses and sympathies are engaged when people seek to express themselves to others. Trying to "read / language in gesture," grasping at foreign words slightly understood, and listening intently to another's translations, the poet discovers that "there's a spirit / has touched us, pulled us / suddenly close" (86).

As topics range from religion and politics to poetry and cellular biology, the question of the relationship of public duty to the individual's creative impulse continually resurfaces. For the American, physically on unfamiliar ground but at home in the experience of sharing knowledge and ideas, the heart of the issue lies in remembering observations by the Russian poet Boris Pasternak. It is the lesson demonstrated in all the outward and inward turning verses of *The Freeing of the Dust*, not simply that one must serve the people, but that "to serve the people in truth one must do . . . / what Pasternak said one must do: *excel oneself / in order to be oneself*" (88). Having traveled a troubling road from antiwar rallies to battlefield hospitals in Vietnam, and through the end of a relationship to the beginning of new ones, Levertov, on the brink of parting from her acquaintances in Moscow, shares and confirms an affirmation of self and community formed steadily throughout this decade of her writing life. When the Russian poet sitting with her "quietly says, and shyly" that "The Poet / never must lose despair" (90), the visiting American and the other listeners, "even the palest spirit among us, burdened / as he is with weight of abstractions," know his meaning. "Smiling / in common knowledge" though separated by nationality, geography, speech,

THE POET IN THE WORLD

and profession, they recognize with the poet that:

we mustn't, any of us, lose touch with the source,
pretend it's not there, cover over
the mineshaft of passion

                       despair somberly tolls its bell
                                 from the depths of,

and wildest joy
sings out of too,

           flashing

                 the scales of its laughing, improbable
                                       music,
grief and delight entwined in the dark down there. (91)

Notes

1. No note accompanied "An Interim" in its initial appearance in *Relearning the Alphabet*. In the brief note that accompanied the poem when it was presented as part of "Staying Alive" in *To Stay Alive*, information was offered in a general way that provided a feel for some historical facts without altering the reader's sense of directly discovering and experiencing the events.

2. Fay Zwicky, "An Interview with Denise Levertov," *Westerly* 2 (July 1979): 125.

3. Reid, "Everyman's Land: Ian Reid Interviews Denise Levertov," *Southern Review* (Adelaide, Australia) 5 (1972): 235.

4. Ernst Cassirer, *The Philosophy of Symbolic Forms Volume Two: Mythical Thought* (New Haven: Yale University Press, 1955) 73, 74.

5. Philip Wheelwright, *The Burning Fountain: A Study in the Language of Symbolism*, new and rev. ed. (Bloomington: Indiana University Press, 1968) 152.

6. The words are reminiscent of Marx's and Engels's "All that is solid melts into air." See Karl Marx and Friedrich Engels, *The Communist Manifesto*, trans. Samuel Moore, introd. A. J. P. Taylor (Harmondsworth, Eng.: Penguin, 1967) 83.

7. Quoted in Denise Levertov, "A Poet's View," *Religion and Intellectual Life* 1 (Summer 1984): 51.

8. Because *To Stay Alive* seems best read as a single work with two organizational units, a group of "Preludes" introducing a long poem in many sections, "Staying Alive," I cite the whole volume rather than individual poems.

9. Conrad Aiken, *Collected Criticism* (London: Oxford UP, 1968) 102.

CHAPTER FIVE

Deciphering the Spirit—People, Places, Prayers: *Life in the Forest, Candles in Babylon, Oblique Prayers, Breathing the Water*

In an interview in February, 1986, for *Sojourners*, Denise Levertov described herself as writing "poetry that articulates engaged emotion and belief." She is not making a completely new appraisal, but the intensity and breadth of the conviction that there are forces larger than man which the poet can experience through the imagination reveals a new spirituality in her treatment of self in relation to other, private perception in relation to public experience. Even if, as Levertov suggests, "my religious faith is at best fragile," she has found in her most recent books that

I also have strongly that sense of so much being "in bud"—so many things being in the beginning of growth, the first shoots of some different consciousness, of moral evolution, despite the fact that we go on more and more effectively doing the awful things that human beings do.

. . . .

. . . there is the deep hope implied in the words, "With God all things are possible."[1]

The publication of *Life in the Forest* in 1978 points the way. Less immediately engaged in politics than the books of the decade preceding it, and by-and-large less intensely self-examining as well, it is a collection of transitions as well as continuations. This book of memories and immediate experiences reveals "not only *what is* but *what might be*" ("Chekhov on the West Heath," *Life* 14) in response, especially, to the death of the poet's mother. As Levertov rediscovers beginnings amidst endings, truths of living as a daughter, mother, lover, writer, teacher, alone and with others, she suggests, as critic Nathan A. Scott, Jr., has written of selfhood, that "not only are we constantly in transit . . . we are conscious of being so."[2]

If *Life in the Forest* takes the poet and the reader toward heightened awareness of a human condition which critic Philip Wheelwright once described as that in which "Man lives always on the verge, always on the borderland of a something more,"[3] the books which follow it, *Candles in Babylon* (1982), *Oblique Prayers* (1984), *Breathing the Water* (1987), take Levertov and her readers over the threshold to new commitments of belief.

Though old notes are sounded in public and private tales of "People, Places, Visions" (*Candles* 41), new chords are struck as well. As central poems of each book suggest, the poet, having looked deeply to see both inner and outer realities, arrives at a kind of spiritual reckoning. She is at a place in her pilgrimage where she offers up not only continuing visions of our dark time, but the light of language and faith. "Oblique Prayers" are voiced in hopes:

> that we may return
> from this place of terror
> home to a calm dawn and
> the work we had just begun.
>> ("Candles in Babylon," *Candles* ix)

Those who have traveled this far with the poet have come not to an ending, but to a recognition in the possibilities of experience of a "happiness / [that] is provisional" ("Of Being," *Prayers* 86), discovered in realizing that though "We live in terror / of what we do not know" "Blesséd is that which utters / its being, / . . . / for there / spirit is" ("Mass for the Day of St. Thomas Didymus," *Candles* 108, 112–13).

Levertov's "Introductory Note" to *Life in the Forest* explains at the outset the book's imaginative terrain, clarifying artistic continuities and suggesting new departures. Having recently discovered in the stark simplicity of Cesare Pavese's poem-stories of the 1930s, *Lavorare Stanca* (*Hard Labor*), "a kind of ratification for a direction" her work "was already obscurely taking," Levertov notes an intention to "try to avoid overuse of the autobiographical, the dominant first-person singular of so much of the American poetry—good and bad—of recent years" (*Life* vii).[4] Yet differences between *Life in the Forest* and *Lavorare Stanca* are also revealing. Not even in "Homage to Pavese," the first section of Levertov's book, does she insist upon what Pavese himself called the "*austerity* of style" or the "close, possessive, passionate adherence to the object" and the "surrendering to the plot"[5] that impelled so many of his poems.

Levertov shares the honesty of Pavese's descriptions, the incisiveness and clarity with which he was able to sketch landscapes and the people who inhabit them.[6] But her narratives, mingling memory, observation, and speculation, define individuals and places not so much by physical limits as by emotional possibilities. Wherever the reader turns in the book he finds "the seed of change" ("Chekhov on the West Heath," *Life* 14), compelling him to see in the account of immediate experiences, a "Continuum" (63) of present, past, and future.

The arrangement of poems in *Life in the Forest*, the poet tells us, is "less chronological than by kind and, within such kinship groups, by internal association from poem to poem" (viii). Levertov's introductory remarks even invite one to take a hand at times in reassembling the shifting shapes that comprise the whole book—suggesting that in moving from section to section readers perceive relationships of tone and structure, if not always direct subject, which bring internal groupings together to span more than one poetic unit. The book's six sections, offering the objectivity of a "Homage to Pavese," as well as a series of personal "Modulations for Solo Voice," range from a descriptive account of the rain and heat of Oaxaca where a seller of serapes makes his endless rounds ("A Mystery [Oaxaca, Mexico]" 21), to the subjective meditations in the entries of a "Metamorphic Journal" (126). But central to the collection, touchstones for the thoughts and emotions of the wide variety of narrative and reflective verses, are the deeply moving group of poems remembering the life and grieving the death of the poet's mother, dying "at home, yet far away from home, / thousands of miles of earth and sea, and ninety years / from her roots" ("A Daughter [I]" 26).

Here Levertov combines meticulous attention to immediate details of person and place with suggestive memories of what once was, or was imagined. She examines, as she has elsewhere, the process by which self and nonself meet in mutual opposition and definition, each becoming other.[7] "Now mother is child, helpless," she observes:

> . . . at the mercy
> of looming figures who have the power
> to move her, feed her, wash her, leave or stay
> at will. And the daughter feels, with horror,
> metamorphosed: *she's* such a looming figure—huge—a
>> tower
> of iron and ice. . . .

>   ("A Daughter [I]" 27)

Exploring the implications of mortality, Levertov maps physical and emotional geographies of intertwined lives, redefining boundaries of physical space and place even as she recognizes and delineates them. And while she finds in anger and despair "love / shrunken in her to a cube of pain / locked in her throat" (27)—experiencing "The way sorrow enters the bone / . . . with stabs and hoverings" ("The Blue Rim of Memory" 93)—the unflinching portrait of her mother's final years presents a picture of life's spirit that will last beyond the moment.

The dying takes place amidst assembled memories, possessions, and sickroom detritus in Mexico where the poet's mother had come late in life. The sights and sounds of the place remind the poet of her mother's failing sensory powers:

> High in the jacaranda shines the gilded thread
> of a small bird's curlicue of song—too high
> for her to see or hear.
> > I've learned
> not to say, these last years,
> "O, look!—O, listen, Mother!"

> > > > ("The 90th Year" 24)

But the immediate sense of loss also reminds the poet of how alive to physical experience the woman had been: "with how much gazing / her life has paid tribute to the world's body!" It reminds the poet as well of just how much she is the inheritor of those gifts of seeing, hearing, caring:

> It was she
> who taught me to look;
> to name the flowers when I was still close to the ground,
> my face level with theirs. . . . (24)

On the brink of parting, the poet envisions the aged woman, her younger self, the adult daughter, and her child self, each image made vivid by the others. In her frustration and weariness, the mother "has written" to her daughter that "I am so tired . . . of appreciating / the gift of life" (25). Still, the juxtaposed views presented here of life budding, in process, diminishing, ending, and continuing, enables the reader to feel the full richness of the gift even as he aches at the inevitable isolation of the dying woman and the survivor, and rages at the grinding slowness with which the aged are turned into brittle husks.

Physically traveling between Boston and Mexico, psychologically and emotionally collapsing space to incorporate vivid remembered or imagined spots of time in Wales and London, Levertov follows her mother's life to "the end of some highway of / factual knowledge, a terminal wall" ("A Daughter [I]" 26). Observing and imagining her mother's final crises, she wrestles with her own doubts, contemplating the nature of identity, commitment, and change. She longs "for her mother to be her mother again":

> consoling, judging, forgiving,

>   whose arms were once
>   strong to hold her and rock her,
>   who used to chant
>   a ritual song that did magic
>   to take away hurt. (27)

But she can perform no magic on the scene herself. Unable "to comfort the child her mother's become," she "briskly, nervously / carries out doctor's orders." Or alone with her thoughts, traveling to and fro "in the air-conditioned sameness of jet-plane efficiency," she "withdraws into lonely distance" (27). Yet from that distance, where the mind can see and stretch physical limit, she is able to imagine:

>   . . . her mother at six years old in the riverfield,
>   twelve years old in her orphan's mourning,
>   twenty, forty, eighty—the storied screen unfolding,
>   told and told—and the days untold. A life!
>   A life—ninetythree years unique in the aeons. (27–28)

Still, Levertov will not delude herself into thinking that through the power of imagining all will be salved. Remembering "herself as a monstrous, tall, swift-moving nurse" ministering to the helpless old woman, she knows her mother's solitude and her own at the end. Recognizing that "she longed to leave . . . / trapped in the house of strangers," Levertov finds that:

>   Something within her twists and turns,
>   she is tired and ashamed. She sobs, but her eyes
>   cannot make tears.

>   ("A Daughter [I]" 28)

> What she wants
> she knows she can't have: one minute
> of communion, here in limbo.
>
> ("A Daugher [II]" 31)

Levertov knows, too, that the physical marks individuals make on their environments, reflections of themselves and their values, rarely outlast them and sometimes disappear beforehand. Three weeks before her mother's death her garden began to vanish, "each day" presenting:

> less sign of the ordered,
> thought-out oasis, a squared circle her mind
> constructed for rose and lily, begonia
> and rosemary-for-remembrance.
> Twenty years in the making—
> less than a month to undo itself. . . .
>
> ("Death in Mexico" 32)

After all, the poet is faced with the recognition that both the dying woman and her writer-daughter are outsiders who have little impact on the indifferent face of things. Her mother's death "was not Mexico's business," though the garden "was a hostage" claimed by "Old gods / [who] took back their own" (33).

The tensions accompanying these realizations are heightened throughout the series of mother-daughter poems by syntactic disruptions and the pressure of mid-line and end-line rhythmic pauses which, playing syntax against halting perceptions and feelings, cause

the lines to move in fits and starts. The reader, forced by
the formal stress to shape the fragments into more complete units of thought, feels in the rough rhythms the
relentless struggle to make coherent sense of the sorrow
and anger that refuses despair:

> A day later begins
> the witnessing. A last week of the dying.
> When she inserts
>   quivering spoonfuls of violently
> green or red *gelatina*
>   into the poor obedient mouth,
> she knows it's futile. . . .
> . . . .
> Each dawn the daughter, shivering,
> opens the curtained door
> and steps out on the balcony; and from time to time
> leans there during the days. Mornings,
> emphatic sunlight seizes the bougainvillea's
> dry magenta blossoms. Among sharp stones, below,
> of the hospital patio,
>   an ugly litter of cigarette stubs
> thrown down by visitors leaning, anxious or bored,
> from other balconies. No one sweeps up.
> Sobs shake her—no tears. She hates
> the uncaring light.
>
> ("A Daughter [II]" 29)

But though Levertov feels the full weight of "Some
force roaming the universe, / malicious and stupid"
which has "affixed . . . / this postscript to so vivid a
life" ("A Daughter [II]" 30), her very re-creation of the
experience sustains that vividness, reaching not only

into the poet's life, but the reader's. The graphic picture
of her mother's last hours offers no comfort:

> She did not die but lies half-speechless, incontinent,
> > aching in body, wandering in mind
> > in a hospital room.
> A plastic tube, taped to her nose,
> > disappears into one nostril.
> Plastic tubes are attached to veins in her arms.
> Her urine runs through a tube into a bottle under the bed.
> On her back and ankles are black sores.
> The black sores are parts of her that have died.
> > ("Death Psalm: O Lord of Mysteries" 39–40)

In her pain, the poet offers up a "Death Psalm" to the
"Lord of mysteries," seeking to reconcile herself to the
fact of "how baffling, how clueless / is laggard death"
which refuses all "dignity of welcome" (39, 40). Although no presence appears out of the darkness to answer the puzzling injustice of lingering death, the poet,
in the very process of looking deeply into the mystery,
not only communicates the harsh reality of old age and
death, but offers a rewarding vision of human experience that lingers as well. Levertov achieves, if not an
answer, at least an honest affirmation of the whole of a
life in the face of an awful picture of its conclusion.

Acknowledging that life is change, sometimes wondrous, sometimes hurtful, the poet seems to confirm in
her act of remembering and formal artistic creation that
a life that was fully lived can still be a living presence to
the uncertain seekers who survive. The woman who
"remembered her griefs. / . . . remembered her hap-
pinesses. / . . . / unfolding the design of her identity"

("Death Psalm" 39), leaves a glimpse of that design which passes into readers' lives. They see it in her acceptance of struggle and her reverence for life, revealed in the way "She tended the green garden she had made," watering daily, fighting off "the destroying ants," and taking note of blossomings (40). They find it in her poignant "unremitting / struggle to learn" ("A Soul-Cake" 41), and in the lessons she marked:

> "To force conscience" . . .
> "is worse," says Castellio, "than cruelly
> to kill a man. For to deny one's convictions
> destroys the soul."
> > And Bruno's lines,
> "The age
> Which I have lived, live, and shall live,
> Sets me atremble, shakes, and braces me." (41–42)

And they find it in her pleasure at play, even in her last months:

Five months before you died you recalled
Counting-rhymes, dance-games for me;
gaily, under the moon, you sang and mimed,

> My shoes are very *dir*ty,
> My shoes are very *thin*,
> I haven't got a *pock*et
> To put a penny in.

> *A soul-cake, a soul-cake,*
> *Please, good missis, a soul-cake* . . . (42)

DECIPHERING THE SPIRIT

Her life, made vivid but deromanticized in the harsh light of her dying, offers readers precisely that, "a soul-cake" for the nourishment of their spirit in being better able to know and accept the reality of their experience of the world.

Elsewhere in *Life in the Forest*, Levertov examines the physical, emotional, and intellectual threads of which a life is woven. Remembering moments spent with a friend on the West Heath, "a section of Hampstead Heath, the tract of never-cultivated land that overlooks London" ("Notes" 34), she recognizes that the past never vanishes into the present, but rather continues to give it shape and definition, both changing and changed by current needs. The past itself was not so much a series of events as a concatenation of partly real, partly imagined, happenings. Personal and public histories, the realities of favorite books and of actual activities, all combined to determine the nature of experience then, as they add to the meaning of the adult poet's life now.

In "Chekhov on the West Heath" Levertov reconstructs the world of "nineteen hundred / and forty-one" (*Life* 10) in which "the dark gauze of youth / swaddled" two friends, "while airraids and news of battle / were part of each ominous day, and in flashes of dread / we glimpsed invasion." However, even with England and Europe apparently "gone down / utterly into the nightmare" (12), the young women found pleasure in their shared experience of place. The vision of it is still vivid to the poet decades later:

> Up from Heath Mansions they go,
> past the long brick wall of the Fenton House garden.
>
> . . . .
>
> the crest of the hill, a stonesthrow of unpaved lane,
> and out to the terrace: a few
> lopsided benches, tussocky grass,
> and the great billowing prospect north.
>
> . . . .
>
> they live! Live
> intensely. Mysterious fragrance
> gentles the air
> under the black poplars. (10–11)

But equally intense, drawing life from place and giving energy to it, were the girls' imagined lives, turning, especially, on the fictive worlds of Anton Chekhov. "Chekhov is with them. / With us" (*Life* 11), Levertov explains: "the Chekhov / who slipped unrecognized into our dreaming days" (13). His stories gave new dimensions to "human measure" as the girls "thrilled to the presence of a power, / unquestioning" (12). What Chekhov would mean to the two, the poet tells her readers, "we still can know only in part." But it is essential to recognize that the meaning, interfused with the broader meaning of the complete experience of the time and place, remains important in the late 1970s. For past and present are not distinct, one giving way to the other: "A place of origin / gives and gives, as we return to it, / bringing our needs" (13).

What "Chekhov on the West Heath" (*Life* 10) "has meant / and goes on meaning, can't be trapped / into

DECIPHERING THE SPIRIT

closed definition. . . . it has to do / not with failure, defeat, frustration" (13), but with "some inkling of rectitude and compassion / . . . breathed in / under the fragrant leaves in wartime London." Places are "built not only of earth but of layers / of human response . . . / in time, in history" (14). Literal and imaginative experiences resonate through the years.

In *Life in the Forest*, a sense of order amidst change marks portraits of "A Son" (100) and of "The Poet Li Po Admiring a Waterfall" (105). It can be felt in the designs of "Blake's Baptismal Font" (108), and in a celebratory vision of "Sunset, Somerville, Late Fall '75" (111). The combination of harmony and flow even more completely defines Levertov's books of the 1980s: *Candles in Babylon*, *Oblique Prayers*, and *Breathing the Water*. As if in momentary completion of the directions of her life's work, Levertov develops her vision of the mysteries of human experience into a statement of religious conviction and faith. As she explained in an article in 1984, "A Poet's View," in *Religion and Intellectual Life*:

all, in the creative act, experience mystery. The concept of "inspiration" presupposes a power which enters the individual and is not a personal attribute; and it is linked to a view of the artist's life as one of obedience to a vocation. David Jones wrote in one of his essays of the artist's impulse to gratuitously set up altars to the unknown god; and I alluded to the passage from what was then an agnostic standpoint. Later, that unknown began to be defined for me as God. . . .

. . . . In the matter of religion . . . I have moved in the last few years . . . to a position of Christian belief. . . . [T]he movement has been . . . gradual and continuous. . . . [8]

When Levertov suggests that "acknowledgment, and celebration, of mystery probably constitutes the most consistent theme of my poetry from its very beginnings," she presents a position "which emphasizes the incapacity of reason alone (much though I delight in elegant logic) to comprehend experience." Because she considers "Imagination the chief of human faculties," she concludes that

It must therefore be by the exercise of that faculty that one moves toward faith, and possibly by its failure that one rejects it as delusion. Poems present their testimony as circumstantial evidences, not as closing argument. Where Wallace Stevens says, "God and the imagination are one," I would say that the imagination, which synergizes intellect, emotion and instinct, is the perceptive organ through which it is possible, though not inevitable, to experience God. [9]

There are also poems in all three of these volumes that are not essentially concerned with issues of belief, in which Levertov continues her explorations of aesthetics, politics, the relationship of self to nonself. Yet even here, more than before, she perceives energies that seem with almost religious power to radiate through and unite experiences. In *Candles in Babylon*, writing of her friend and mentor William Carlos Williams whose work has been too often linked almost exclusively to his "no ideas but in things" proclamation in *Paterson*,[10] Levertov makes clear that "There are many more 'ideas' in William Carlos Williams' 'things' than he is commonly credited with even today."[11] He does not present "the bald image" in his poems; rather, he reveals "a mind / secret, disciplined, generous and / unfathomable," "lodged / among the words" of his verses, "undulant, elusive, beyond reach / of any dull / staring eye" ("Williams: An Essay," *Candles* 59).

Levertov suggests that Williams "loved / persistence," but believed it must be "linked to invention." He prized not simply what the eye could see, but what imagination and sight together might envision: "He loved / the lotus cup, fragrant / upon the swaying water," but loved, too, "the wily mud / pressing swart riches into its roots, / and the long stem of connection" (*Candles* 60).

Writing "In Memory of Muriel Rukeyser," her "great intelligent friend" (*Candles* 91), Levertov is able to conjure "the passion for life, the vision / of love and work" (90) that marked Rukeyser in life, and is sustained in the spiritual power of her still-living presence: "Now. Stop shaking. Imagine her. / She was a cathedral" (91). And in offering a psalm in praise of "People Power at the Die-in" (84), she pays tribute to a sense that:

> great power flowed from us,
> luminous, a promise. Yes! . . .
>
> great energy flowed from solitude,
> and great power from communion. (85)

Even "Pig Dreams" (23), Levertov's playful series of verses outlining the days and ways of "Sylvia . . . faithful / Petpig, teacher / of humans, fount / of pig-wisdom," ends with a grand vision of harmony and promise as "Isis Speaks" to her faithful charge of what awaits after her life among humans. Promising that "in springtimes to come / your black hide shall be strewn / with constellations of blossom," the goddess envisions a spiritual dwelling place where Sylvia will be revered, living "long, and at peace, / redreaming the lore of your destiny" ("Isis Speaks, *Candles* 40).

But Levertov's ambitious long poem, "Mass for the Day of St. Thomas Didymus" (*Candles* 108), offers the clearest view of the force of her new beliefs. The figure of the Apostle Thomas, the doubting Thomas of the Gospel According to John, is in many ways an ideal choice to reveal the nature of Levertov's faith. For in making demands for physical proof of Jesus' resurrection, confirming his belief only after declaring his incredulity, he drew forth the crucial response which illuminates the gospel and seems to underlie Levertov's poem: "Have you believed because you have seen me? Blessed are those who have not seen and yet believe" (John 20.29).

A basic given of Levertov's six-part poem is that individuals "live in terror / of what [they] know," imagining "death, death, and the world's / death." But they live in greater terror "of what [they] do not know, / in terror of not knowing" (*Candles* 108). Yet as the poet declares in the opening "Kyrie" section of her "Mass,"

DECIPHERING THE SPIRIT

her plea for mercy, "our hope lies" precisely "in the unknown, / in our unknowing." Applying Thomas's lesson, those who are not able to comprehend the force that flows through the world, but are aware of it, must believe its presence and power nonetheless. Thus Levertov moves her reader from the prayer that the "deep, remote unknown, / . . . / Have mercy upon us" to a hymn of appreciation in her second section, "Gloria." Here she bids her audience: "Praise / . . . the unknown" which:

> . . . gives us
> still,
> in the shadows of death,
>   our daily life,
>   and the dream still
> of goodwill, of peace on earth. (109)

She offers praise for "flow and change," for "night and / the pulse of day" (109).

At the middle of her poetic liturgy, Levertov presents her own "Credo" in place of the Nicene Creed, clarifying further her complex faith and its relationship to the example of the Apostle Thomas:

> I believe the earth
> exists, and
> in each minim mote
> of its dust the holy
> glow of thy candle.
>
> . . . .
> . . . I believe and

> interrupt my belief with
> doubt. I doubt and
> interrupt my doubt with belief. Be,
> belovéd, threatened world.

(*Candles* 110)

The "Sanctus" that follows, Levertov's naming of all that is holy, hymns the God-given human power of imagination to comprehend harmonies even while admitting anxiety and doubt. Here, with a bell-like ringing chant of praise, "sanctus, hosanna, sanctus," the poet proclaims the importance of "all that Imagination / has wrought, has rendered," all the varied forms of God and religion it has named and made in the effort to grasp "the Vast Loneliness" of the world, comprehending it, shaping it in the process, giving it "a hearth, a locus" and thereby making it manageable. As the poet exclaims, "all the gods, / angels and demigods, eloquent animals, oracles, / storms of blessing and wrath," products of the imagination "striving, in throes of epiphany—/ naming, forming," all

> send forth their song towards
> the harboring silence, uttering
> the ecstasy of their names, the multiform
> name of the Other, the known
> Unknown, unknowable. . . . (111)

For Levertov, as her "Benedictus" suggests, "Blesséd is that which comes in the name of the spirit, / that which bears / the spirit within it" (*Candles* 111). The spirit is in "that which utters / its being" (112), in any-

DECIPHERING THE SPIRIT

one who, seeking to comprehend the world, finds a self. Perhaps it exists most prominently in the artist's commitment and vision, her ability to find words which begin to express human limit and achievement. "The word," Levertov reminds her readers, "chose to become / flesh. In the blur of flesh / we bow, baffled" (113), humbled before the magic of transubstantiation and before inevitable frailties. After all, perhaps weaknesses are saving strengths. The capacity to doubt and fret and love gathers not in omnipotence, but in hard-earned conviction. Man is willing both to give over to an awesome power and to offer "something human"—the power of caring—to "shield" (115) the "Lamb of God" (113), which is thereby revealed to him in the very act of compassion and engagement.

In the different parts of her "Mass," and throughout *Candles in Babylon*, Levertov affirms struggle, hope, a capacity for imaginative vision—the mortal capabilities that enable us to grasp and reach toward the immortal. "For that the vision / was given to me," she declares: "to know and share, / passing from hand to hand, although / its clarity dwindles in our confusion" ("The Many Mansions" 116). Levertov feels that the poet's capacity to see and express coherence in the commonplace and beyond it reveals "the amulet of mercy" to a troubled world, calming confusion without denying it. Having borrowed again from John for the title of this last poem in *Candles in Babylon*, Levertov confirms for those whose faith is not easy that there are indeed "Many Mansions" in God's "house,"[12] places for all manner and degrees of belief.

Despite such confirmation, however, Levertov is propelled at times by her conflict of belief and doubt into a troubling neutral zone of the spirit, not a "profound *dark / night of the soul*," but a gray "place / without clear outlines" ("Oblique Prayer," *Prayers* 82). To this, she responds with a book of *Oblique Prayers* (1984). Seeking to retain a vision of "the blessèd light that caressed the world" before she "stumbled into / this place of mere / not-darkness" (*Prayers* 83), the poet organizes her book into four sections that define the threatening darkness and grayness, and embrace the brightness of faith. In the first sections, she moves the reader through what is by now familiar territory. She provides "Decipherings" (1) of the routines, stresses, and hopes of daily experience in places as disparate as London and Ohio. Too, she offers insight into the various ways individuals are "Prisoners" (27) of violent history in Lebanon or El Salvador. By way of immediate response, in the final two sections she explores the nature "Of God and of the Gods" (69) with her own spiritual speculations and with her translations of fourteen poems by Frenchman Jean Joubert, with whom she has powerful sympathies of sound, sight, and spirit.

In a recent essay entitled " 'Gathered at the River': Background and Form," in which she describes the making of a poem that re-creates and meditates upon a 1982 memorial observance of the bombing of Hiroshima and Nagasaki, Levertov expresses the idea that

"sin" occurs when humans violate the wellbeing of their own species and other living things, denying the natural law, the interdependence of all. . . .

My underlying belief in a great design, a potential harmony which can be violated or be sustained, probably strikes some people as quaint; but I would be dishonest, as a person and artist, if I disowned it.[13]

The translations from Jean Joubert's *Cinquante toiles pour un espace blanc* (Paris: Grasset, 1982), which she introduces to an American public in the third section of *Oblique Prayers*, offer a nearly perfect vehicle for her to confirm the conviction of design, suggesting that it is not simply her own "quaint" obsession. "Brilliant Sky" and "The Poet's Late Autumn," the final two poems, are particularly telling. For here, confronting the reality of "a friend . . . entering his death" ("Brilliant Sky," *Prayers* 65), Joubert discovers, as Levertov has, the light of harmony and coherence in the darkest moment.

Earlier, pondering the question "Are We Ruled by the Wind?" Joubert had walked a familiar landscape able to "sense the vibration / of bonds that wed me / to the great host of invisible stars." Like Levertov, who was able to perceive the feeling of "so many things being in the beginning of growth,"[14] the Frenchman senses that

. . . everywhere sap is rising
in tree after tree, and flows
in the very veins of the garden towards me, and bathes
the palms of my hands.

(Prayers 63)

The answer to the problem stated in the title of the poem seems to lie in recognizing that man neither rules nor is "ruled by the wind," possibilities which would suggest relationships of power and control. Rather, he participates with the wind in a kind of natural continuum, giving a degree of wholeness to, and being completed by, the design:

> Early light
> burnishes a web's perfection
> where the archangel keeps vigil. Together
> we pray, in silence
> receive, accept
> the immense breathing which laves us. (63)

As the poet Stanley Kunitz wrote in a lecture on the poet and state, "Man will perish unless he learns that the web of the universe is a continuous tissue. Touch it at any point, and the whole web shudders."[15] In "Brilliant Sky," Joubert's intense painterly meditation on living and dying, "the whole web shudders." The poem is reminiscent of Coleridge's "This Lime-Tree Bower My Prison" in suggesting that a common view of the vast sky can draw together and comfort separated friends who, despite their apparent isolation, share a glimpse of a design larger than the individual self. But it reaches farther in its vision of coherence, confronting not only imprisoning absence, but pending death.

More immediately, confidently, and intensely than Coleridge, Joubert proffers a vision of man's potential at-oneness with the natural world. Whereas Coleridge's meditator moves haltingly from a vision of a place that

is "narrow, deep, / And only speckled by the mid-day
sun" to the sight of "the mighty Orb's dilated glory"[16]
before which he and his absent friend stand gazing,
Joubert's observer, his vision of the sky momentarily ob-
scured by branches, perceives his situation in an instant
as one of invitation, not separation. The natural obstacle
to perception seems to heighten it:

> Never between the branches has the sky
> burned with such brilliance, as if
> it were offering all of its light to me,
> as if it were trying to speak to me. . . .
>
> (*Prayers* 65)

Seeming to take its cue from the human witness, the
winter sky, personified as a "transparent mouth,"
strains with energy in an effort to communicate an "urgent mystery." Seen through a geometry of bare
branches in the "cold emptiness and silence" of winter,
it seems to be breaking free of restriction: "the air / suddenly arches itself . . . into infinity, / and glitters" (65).
And in the discharge of electric force that surrounds the
solitary speaker, announcing his active interrelationship
with the living universe, he envisions a friend who,
though dying, is part of the moment too. The "mystery" which the intertwined winter landscape and
mindscape seems to reveal is one of continuity, harmony, and release. However cold and empty the winter
view might have been, it is not a frozen scene. Rather it

is radiant with brightness, motion, and sharing, despite its sadness:

> This evening, far from here,
> a friend is entering his death,
> he knows it, he walks
> under bare trees alone,
> perhaps for the last time. So much love,
> so much struggle, spent and worn thin.
> But when he looks up, suddenly the sky
> is arrayed in this same vertiginous clarity. (65)

Joubert's encounter with death and the natural world is clarified still further in "The Poet's Late Autumn," Levertov's final selection of his work for *Oblique Prayers*. Quietly observing that "Each morning, making tea, / I think of my dead friend" (*Prayers* 65), the poet faces and communicates both his sorrow and his increasingly clear sense of his own place in the natural design. Acknowledging his feeling of solitude and his sense of loss, he refutes isolation with an awareness of the presence in his life of forces of change and continuity beyond any individual's control. Even in his feelings of deep separateness, he discovers a broad plan and harmony of which he is a part:

> I am alone, I write nothing,
>   I thank
> the gods for this great breadth
>   of empty light.

> At times, over the hills a jet
> leaves a white trail
> a lofty wind
>   slowly unravels. (67)

The reader has already seen that like Joubert's spirituality, Levertov's often seems centered on perceptions of man in relation to the natural world. But though Levertov is sympathetic to his revelation of man's place in nature's design, her final section of *Oblique Prayers* reveals a faith that is more directly Christian than pantheistic. As she has said in an interview recently, "Maybe my Christianity is unorthodox, but it's still a Christian unorthodoxy."[17] In the poem "This Day," Levertov reflects upon a time in which she takes communion, tastes "Dry wafer, / sour wine." One might expect the ritual enactment of sharing simply to confirm order, but the poet finds herself, rather, peering more deeply into confusion:

> This day I see
>
> God's in the dust,
> not sifted
>
> out from confusion.
>
>   (*Prayers* 80)

As an artist and an observer of the world, Levertov seeks a resolution to her bewilderment in both everyday sights and in the world of art as these reveal points of entry into spiritual understanding. Even commonplaces seem fraught with a peculiar melodrama, reflecting the speaker's state of mind. Passing a duckpond she notes the swirl of confusion in what might seem to be a calm scene. The small pool seems a microcosm of larger disruptions, "brilliantly somber water / deranged by lost feathers and bits of / drowning bread." Perhaps, though, the poet ponders, "these imperfections" are inseparable from a more satisfying whole:

> are part of perfection,
> a pristine nuance? our eyes,
> our lives, too close to the canvas,
> enmeshed within
> the turning dance,
> to see it?

> (*Prayers* 80)

If everyday scenes themselves seem to capture an essential blend of comfort and discomfort, confusion and design, art offers even more explicitly "a visible quietness" amidst anxiety and doubt. Meditating later in the poem upon realistic "Dutch 17th-century paintings" (*Prayers* 80), Levertov marks the ways they represent the civilizing impact of human activities upon life's disharmonies, observing in the paintings "the concord / of lute and harpsichord" and the repose of "a smiling conversation" that generates and represents "calme, luxe" (80–81) in a domestic interior. But she notes, too, in a question that seems to be answered in the very fact of its utterance, that the orderly calm extends far beyond the idea that civilized activities can tame disorder and disharmony. The Dutch artists, it appears, revealed harmony in the most common objects of their worlds as well as in the objects that civilized arts and artifices might transform:

> . . . also the clutter
> of fruit and herbs, pots, pans, poultry,
> strewn on the floor: and isn't
> the quiet upon them too, in them and of them,
> aren't they wholly at one with the wonder? (81)

For Levertov, the "wonder," whether found in nature or in art, reflects the full range of experiences. On "This Day" (80) of sacrament Levertov has come to see "the world, a word / intricately incarnate" which "offers—/ . . . / what hunger craves." She finds a faith which, refusing to deny confusion or difference, acknowledges both the common and the transcendent, and enables the individual to be "at one with the wonder" (81) in all its disturbing and invigorating variety.

Levertov ends *Oblique Prayers* with three radiantly confident poems of gratitude and praise. Simply and directly she celebrates connection, a "happiness" which though "provisional" is accompanied by "An awe so quiet / I don't know when it began."[18] Accepting without qualification her need to create and to be part of the whole fabric of a larger creation, "this need to dance, / this need to kneel: / this mystery" ("Of Being" 86), Levertov, after a long pilgrimage of commitment and belief, discovers "A gratitude / had begun to sing in me" ("Understanding" 85). With biblical echoes, resonance, and rhetoric, she declares in "Passage" (87), the book's final poem, the truth of her own long passage as a poet. She recognizes that a spirit of holiness is made manifest in the many surfaces of the perceptible world. It spins space and time together into an intricate fabric and brightens our gaze. All of living creation is engaged and defined by the force of it. "The spirit that walked upon the face of the waters," Levertov writes, "walks the meadow of long grass; / green shines to silver where the spirit passes":

> The grasses numberless, bowing and rising, silently
> cry hosanna as the spirit
> moves them and moves burnishing
>
> over and again upon mountain pastures
> a day of spring, a needle's eye
> space and time are passing through like a swathe of silk.
>
> (87)

In one of her earliest books Levertov proclaimed the special magic of the poet's relation to the natural world by hinting that in her presence readers might go *Overland to the Islands* (1958). Now, almost thirty years later, more comfortable than ever in her role as a magician with words, she suggests further that in the world she imagines most things are possible, even *Breathing the Water* (1987).

Levertov's final volume to date is a wonderfully made book of reconstructions and transformations. Making old material new, the poet looks back to earlier

DECIPHERING THE SPIRIT

poems and subjects, and again uses as a springboard
the work of Rilke. She discovers new inspirations as
well, meditating upon a religious painting by Spaniard
Diego Velázquez (1599–1660), reshaping a moment of
early Christian poet Caedmon's history as recounted by
the medieval English scholar Bede, and "spinning off"
verse based on photographs by Peter McAfee Brown, a
letter by contemporary religious poet Thomas Merton, a
sermon by Father Benignus in Stanford, California.[19] In
some of the finest lyrics of the book, Levertov offers
readings of pieces of Englishwoman Julian of Norwich's
fourteenth-century book of divine revelations or *Showings*. Throughout *Breathing the Water*, in an effort to reveal the interrelationship of physical life and spiritual,
Levertov demonstrates the transforming power of the
poet's imagination over both literary and natural
objects.

Her book begins and ends with poems that are variations on themes found in Rilke's *Book of Hours*. These
two transformations, together with a third that appears
very near the end of *Breathing the Water*, form a kind of
frame around the whole, illuminating Levertov's subjects, intentions, and techniques. Taking off from the
poems that inspired them, the verses offer meditations,
extensions, commentaries, upon the originals. Introducing a 1960 edition of Rilke's *Selected Works*, translator
J. B. Leishman gave a useful explanation of the origin of
book 1 of the *The Book of Hours*, the meditations of a
Russian monk. Paraphrasing and quoting from Rilke's
letter of May 14, 1911, to Marlise Gerding, "who had

presumably asked him in what sense it was to be regarded as 'religious'," Leishman wrote:

He declared that, at a time when he was occupied with other tasks, words, "prayers, if you like", suddenly began to come to him. . . . The act of writing them down strengthened and summoned inspiration. . . . Rilke then proceeds to declare that all piety is either inexplicable or indifferent to him that does not contain something of invention, and that, for him, our relationship to God presupposes a certain "creativity", a certain "inventive genius."[20]

Sharing the conviction that exercise of the imagination defines in large measure one's relationship with God, Levertov applies her own "inventive genius" to the observations and declarations of Rilke's monk. She acknowledges and celebrates man's creative relationship to nature. Sharpening the softly suggestive music of Rilke's symbolist musings, where sounds rather than statements or objects convey meaning, Levertov firmly places the spiritual in the physical. Instead of shimmering implications she offers solid architectural substance, articulating a world both concrete and transcendent.

Consider the first poem in *Breathing the Water* along with its source. The first stanza of the first poem of *The Book of Hours*, the piece Levertov selected for her initial "Variation on a Theme by Rilke," vibrates with elusive moods and meanings:

With strokes that ring clear and metallic, the hour
to touch me bends down on its way:

> my senses are quivering. I feel I've the power—
> and I seize on the pliable day.[21]

By contrast, Levertov's poem describes the moment more directly and in detail, though meaning remains suggestive:

> A certain day became a presence to me;
> there it was, confronting me—a sky, air, light:
> a being. And before it started to descend
> from the height of noon, it leaned over
> and struck my shoulder as if with
> the flat of a sword, granting me
> honor and a task. The day's blow
> rang out, metallic—or it was I, a bell awakened,
> and what I heard was my whole self
> saying and singing what it knew: *I can.*
>
> (*Breathing* 3)

Rilke's unspecified setting, a philosophic hovering in time and space, has become a specific, albeit still somewhat generalized, incident of vision. It happens on "A certain day" at a precise time—"the height of noon"—when "sky, air, light" gather together to reveal in their energy and harmony a presence or "being" in the world that is larger than an individual self. The poem's active, almost violent, diction ("struck," "sword," "blow," "rang out, metallic") suggests the power of the vision, and the completeness of the surrender to it. But even the images of confrontation and battle depict control as well as the release of highly charged energy. The speaker is struck by the wonder of the day, not destructively, but "as if with / the flat of a sword" in some chivalric ritual of design and order "granting . . . / honor and a task" of enabling others to share the vision of wholeness. In the moment, Levertov discovers that the sense of outer coherence, confidence, and force, radiates equally from within, a spirit that flows through all creation, heard in the ringing of "The day's blow" and in the poet's "whole self" "singing . . . *I can.*"

The precise nature of the poet's visionary "task" is further elaborated in the second of Levertov's variations on a theme by Rilke. Placed late in *Breathing the Water*, her response to book 1, poem 4 of *The Book of Hours* serves as a kind of summation of the role of the artist as a perceiver and communicator of divine mystery in the natural world. Whereas Rilke's monk cautiously announces human limit in representing images of the divine in nature, stressing restriction and control as primary functions of perception, Levertov's speaker suggests an opening out of the spirit and imagination, accenting once again the correlation of individual insight and the world outside the self. "We dare not paint you at our own dictation," Rilke's cleric observes of the "maiden-dawn from whom the morning grew." Trusting neither their senses nor their individual capacities for accurate perception, Rilke's observers gather representations "From pigments of an older generation," "those strokes, the same irradiation / with which long since the saint secreted you." Although reverence for the works and images of past masters is in some sense an affirmation of achievement and continuity, it suggests here, too, a failure of confidence and an unwill-

ingness to respond with eye and emotion to the wonder
before one. With vision "open to [their] hearts," some
choose instead to veil their sight:

> We've built up images like walls before you,
> till now you're hemmed with thousands of ramparts.
> For to your veils our pious hands restore you
> whenever you are open to our hearts.[22]

But for the monk who speaks in Levertov's "Variations on a Theme by Rilke (*The Book of Hours*, Book I,
Poem 4)" art offers a multiplicity of truths, each image
opening a way into the comprehension of the divine.
The austere simplicity of the Christ of fourteenth-
century Italian painter Giotto, the softer radiance of
fifteenth-century Dutch master Van Eyck's, the graphic
realism of Dutchman Rembrandt's in the seventeenth
century, the expressive sadness and harsh anger of
Frenchman Georges Rouault's darkly lined modernist
vision in the twentieth century, are all "true"[23]:

> not one is a fancy, a willed fiction,
> each of them shows us exactly
> the manifold countenance
> of the Holy One, Blessed be He.

> (*Breathing* 71)

Images of God change as men and perspectives change,
and the imagination, embracing multiplicity, keeps the
reader in touch with the moving spirit.

Levertov's monk suggests, further, that more func-
tional architectural art, designed to erect changeless

monuments to faith, reveals the interactive nature of spirituality that links inner worlds to outer, individuals to a grand design. Considering the structures men build in the name of religion, Levertov envisions not the restrictive walls and ramparts in Rilke's verse, but manmade constructions that release space and collapse protective barriers. After all, her speaker ponders rhetorically, "[aren't both] The seraph buttress flying / to support a cathedral's external walls" and "the shadowy ribs of the vaulted sanctuary / . . . equally . . . / the form of a holy place?" (*Breathing* 71).

The interfusion of interior spaces and exterior ones is perhaps most visible in the play of light through the "ruby / and celestial sapphire" of church windows which "can be seen / only from the inside, but then / only when light enters from without." The patterns individuals shape to express connection with the Infinite must wait upon the uncontrollable movement of natural forces to reveal their intensity, express their completeness. The makers of art cannot dominate their forms but must be receptive to the changing external shape of things, which will inevitably affect their creations. Levertov makes clear that all true artists are linked through time to their fellows. Yet more important still is the recognition that man's creativity is dependent upon God's:

> From the divine twilight, neither dark nor day,
> blossoms the morning. . . .
> . . . Thus the Infinite

plays, and in grace
gives us clues to His mystery.

(Breathing 71)

Levertov's "Variation and Reflection on a Theme by
Rilke (*The Book of Hours*, Book I, Poem 7)" (*Breathing* 83)
also gives the reader "clues." This last poem of the book
sounds a cautionary note, urging him to recognize the
necessity for a kind of negative capability, the capacity
to remain open to a spiritual experience that will not be
delimited despite the reader's powerful formal urge toward closure and completion. Though restless, readers
must recognize that they can neither abandon nor solve
"His mystery." Clarifying and elaborating upon Rilke's
abstract reflection that one might gratefully discover
harmony in the world "If only stillness reigned, pure,
elemental,"[24] Levertov explains what such quiet might
entail. Freed from the fretfulness of daily action and
thought that keeps one bustling, bound up in "casual
events," one might discover the power of the human
mind to shape a kind of cosmic coherence. No longer
yoked to "the swing of cause and effect," men might be
gods, moving beyond themselves to conquer and control their environments. "If just for once," Levertov
writes, "the swing of cause and effect, / cause and effect, / would come to rest":

then my thought, single and multifold,
could think you into itself
until it filled with you to the very brim,
bounding the whole flood of your boundlessness:

> and at that timeless moment of possession,
> fleeting as a smile, surrender you
> and let you flow back into all creation.

(*Breathing* 83)

But offering a "Reflection" as well as a "Variation" on Rilke, Levertov suggests that such absolute calm is not only impossible for humans, but inappropriate and even undesirable, for it falsifies the human condition. And yet, although "There will never be that stillness," lives are charged with the gleam of a visionary grandeur:

> Within the pulse of flesh,
> in the dust of being, where we trudge,
>   turning our hungry gaze this way and that,
> the wings of the morning
> brush through our blood. . . .

(*Breathing* 83)

Humankind is laved in light, clear sight, and energy, as well as in the frustrating realization of human limit. The poet suggests that "What we desire travels with us"; and man the adaptable animal, alive in a world of change, "must breathe time as fishes breathe water." Accepting the flow as his natural element, moving with it rather than being defeated by it, he will see with the poet a spiritual plan, realizing that in our very restlessness "God's flight circles us" (*Breathing* 83).

With the early and late variations on Rilke marking a thematic and perceptual boundary for *Breathing the*

DECIPHERING THE SPIRIT

Water, Levertov maps her poetic territory throughout the volume with poems that further explore the relationship of art to belief, observation to vision, self to spirit. Many of the verses are transformations, as the Rilke poems were. Permitting echoes and fragments of sources to resonate audibly and visibly through new verbal constructs, Levertov creates an energy born of recognizing continuity and change together.

Like the "Spinoffs" (*Breathing* 85) from photographs and snatches of reading which Levertov presents in two groups of short lyrics in *Breathing the Water*, but more completely linked to their source, these transformations are spun off from a particular original. While "A 'spinoff' . . . is a verbal construct which neither describes nor comments but moves off at a tangent to, or parallel with, its inspiration" (85–86), these transformations tend to be descriptive *and* commentative *and* to move off in a variety of parallel and tangential ways from their inspiration. Most illuminating are four which recount the nature of revelation: "The Servant-Girl at Emmaus" (66), which takes as its source a Velázquez painting; "Caedmon" (65), which is gathered from Bede's *An Ecclesiastical History of the English People*; and two drawn from Julian of Norwich's *Showings*, "On a Theme from Julian's Chapter XX" (68) and "The Showings: Lady Julian of Norwich, 1342–1416" (75).

Levertov's eye and imagination seem to have been caught not only by the subject of Velázquez's early (*c*.1620) painting drawn from Saint Luke's account of the resurrected Christ on the road to Emmaus,[25] but by a quirky fact in the painting's history. Velázquez's portrait of a startled black servant girl looking deeply attentive to, though not looking at, a scene taking place behind her as she performs her kitchen tasks, was cleaned in 1933 to reveal a small corner background scene of Christ taking a meal at the village of Emmaus. The unexpected appearance of the diners, suddenly clarifying the woman's expression and attitude of discovery, contributes a surprising twist to the painting's representation of what Luke defined as a distinction between perception and recognition. The viewer can now perceive and ponder what the kitchen maid recognizes: the presence of Christ on earth. The cleaned canvas also offers a clear picture of Velázquez's idea of the relationship of the human and the divine. Focusing less immediately upon the figure of Christ than upon his impact on the common people, the painter details a moment described only generally in Luke:

they constrained him, saying, "Stay with us, for it is toward evening and the day is now far spent." So he went in to stay with them. When he was at table with them, he took the bread and blessed and broke it, and gave it to them. And their eyes were opened and they recognized him; and he vanished out of their sight. (Luke 24.29–31)

By filling in the scene and making it realistic, crowding the foreground with familiar objects to occupy our primary attention while Christ's dinner takes place in smaller scale at a distance and off to one side of the

DECIPHERING THE SPIRIT

canvas, Velázquez suggests that immediate recognition of the divine takes place in the world of everyday occurrences.

Taking off from the visual image to speculate upon what the young servant girl might be feeling, Levertov also clarifies the reader's understanding of the way the senses and faith combine to reveal the spiritual in the physical. While "Those who had brought this stranger home to their table / don't recognize yet with whom they sit," the girl combines belief with a capacity to listen and to see the world about her. She not only perceives the sights and sounds of her environment, she comprehends them. Levertov's chantlike repetitions of words and phrases, together with frequent rhythmic hesitations that interrupt lines, convey the nervous intensity of the moment of perception and discovery:

She listens, listens, holding
her breath. Surely that voice
is his—the one
who had looked at her, once, across the crowd,
as no one ever had looked?
Had seen her? Had spoken as if to her?

"Surely those hands were his," the speaker thinks, "Surely that face—?"

Those who had brought this stranger home to their table
don't recognize yet with whom they sit.
But she in the kitchen, absently touching
                    the winejug she's to take in,[26]
a young Black servant intently listening,

swings round and sees
the light around him
and is sure.

(Breathing 66)

Of course the final action, the swinging around to
confirm the initial understanding of the senses and
the emotional desire to believe, takes place just after the
frozen moment of the painting. Levertov imagines the
reward of certitude, of being "sure," for acts of attention
and faith; thus the mystery of spirit is revealed, still
alive in the world.

If "The Servant-Girl at Emmaus" suggests the
power of vision felt through the senses and caught by
the painter's art, "Caedmon" reveals even more dramatically a miraculous intertwining of sense and spirit.
Noting that the poem "forms a companion piece to 'St.
Peter and the Angel' in *Oblique Prayers*' " (*Breathing* 86),
Levertov presents in first person narration a retelling of
the Venerable Bede's history of how an illiterate peasant
miraculously received the gift of song. Where "St. Peter
and the Angel" spins off from the biblical description in
the Acts of the Apostles of Peter's rescue from prison by
the appearance of God's angel, "Caedmon" shifts the
focus of sensory response and belief from sight and
touch to sound.

Describing Peter's miraculous escape, the narrator
of Acts writes:

behold, an angel of the Lord appeared, and a light
shone in the cell; and he struck Peter on the side and

DECIPHERING THE SPIRIT

woke him, saying, "Get up quickly." And the chains
fell off his hands. . . . he did not know that what was
done by the angel was real, but thought he was seeing
a vision. . . . and they went out and passed on
through one street; and immediately the angel left
him. And Peter came to himself, and said, "Now I am
sure that the Lord has sent his angel and rescued me."
(Acts 12.7–11)

Levertov's imaginative response, suggesting with the
narrator of Acts that the spirit made manifest *is* real,
also suggests that belief in the spiritual actuality of what
the eye may perceive constitutes both a burden and a
release. The discovery of the freedom of a faith linked
to, but expanding, physical experience, is both exhilirat-
ing and terrifying. "Delivered out of raw continual pain,
/ smell of darkness, groans of those others / to whom he
was chained," Levertov's St. Peter is led with "one hand
on the angel's shoulder, one / feeling the air before him,
/ eyes open but fixed." He recognizes only when the
angel has left him "alone and free" that "this was no
dream." The acceptance of miracle, dependent on imaginative and sympathetic response to experience which
cannot be reasonably explained, is "More frightening /
than arrest, than being chained to his warders," for it
brings one face to face with the recognition of human
limit and promise: "He himself must be / the key, now,
to the next door, / the next terrors of freedom and joy"
(*Prayers* 79).

Visual and tactile sensations are an important part
of the description of miracle in Levertov's version of

Caedmon's tale as well. But they seem gathered there to point toward a different miracle that reveals man's link to a spiritual presence. Describing his visionary moment, the Christian singer who was once a cowherd explains that

> The cows
> munched or stirred or were still. I
> was at home and lonely,
> both in good measure. Until
> the sudden angel affrighted me—light effacing
> my feeble beam,
> a forest of torches, feathers of flame, sparks upflying. . . .
>
> (*Breathing* 65)

The rhythmic power in the heavy alliterative stresses is reminiscent of Caedmon's original Old English verse: "affrighted," "effacing," "feeble," "forest," "feathers," "flame," "upflying." Surrounding her readers with thumping sonic energy and noisy words that bespeak motion—"torches," "feathers," "flame," "upflying," "touched," "scorched," "pulled"—Levertov leads them to a statement that confirms in both its kinesthetic manner and matter the visionary impact of the sound sense:

> . . . nothing was burning,
> nothing but I, as that hand of fire
> touched my lips and scorched my tongue
> and pulled my voice
> into the ring of the dance. (65)

DECIPHERING THE SPIRIT

Suggesting that spirit, word, music, and dance are inevitably linked, Levertov's "Caedmon" reveals man in active, creative harmony with himself and with forces beyond the self. But Levertov's long poem "The Showings: Lady Julian of Norwich, 1342–1416" (*Breathing* 75), and its companion piece, "On a Theme from Julian's Chapter XX" (68), explore most completely the relationship of the human and the divine, body and spirit, drawing upon the visionary prose of an Englishwoman who lived the solitary life of an anchoress near the Church of St. Julian, Conisford, Norwich.[27] Here Levertov not only recreates moments of the mystical experience recounted in Julian's spiritual autobiography, but enters into a dialogue with the remarkable medieval woman, contemplating the nature of knowledge and seeking to reconcile human limitation with the mysteries of faith.

Opening "The Showings" with a direct address that establishes a kind of intimacy through time between poet and mystic, Levertov takes full measure of the different worlds they inhabit. While science clarifies for the modern woman, faith certifies for the medieval woman. Yet Levertov suggests that perhaps more than five-hundred years of information gathering has brought humankind, finally, as much to a knowledge of what it doesn't know as to a picture of what it does. Explaining "things-as-they-are" to her companion of the imagination, drawing a contrast between present and past, Levertov raises the possibility that older recognitions, accessible through belief, imagination, and desire, may be as true or truer than those reason has defined. Itemizing the complexity of our modern knowing and our failure to know, she observes to Julian that "there are vast gaps we call black holes, / unable to picture what's both dense and vacant":

> and there's the dizzying multiplication of all
> language can name or fail to name, unutterable
> swarming of molecules. All Pascal
> imagined he could not stretch his mind to imagine
> is known to exceed his dread.

> > *(Breathing* 75)

The confusions of trying to know such a variety of life viewed under the microscope, or telescope, are multiplied by the astonishing variety of immediate impressions that constitutes daily experience in our time:

> And there's the earth of our daily history,
> its memories, its present filled with the grain
> of one particular scrap of carpentered wood we happen
> to be next to, its waking light on one especial leaf,
> this word or that, a tune in this key not another,
> beat of our hearts *now*, good or bad,
> dying or being born, eroded, vanishing. . . .

> > *(Breathing* 75)

Against this welter of experience to measure, Julian's perception in her *Showings* seems impossibly naive, asking as it does from a seemingly simpler world that humankind "turn [its] gaze / inside out" so that it is able to see *"a little thing, the size of a hazelnut,* and believe / it is our world." Can it be, Levertov ponders rhetorically, that man is asked to accept this microcosm as one which "encompasses / every awareness our minds contain," and that "All limitless space" is "given form in this / medieval enigma"? No observed fact of experience will allow this, of course, but the poet accepts the riddle as a "sharing" of the "mystery" of *all that is made*" (*Breathing* 75), a truth of spirit and imagination rather than of mind and measure. What Julian sees seems to be "our world" not for what it is, but for what it represents to the imagining perceiver: the creating and loving presence of God. As Julian writes in the fourth chapter of her *Showings*:

He showed me something small, no bigger than a hazelnut, lying in the palm of my hand. . . . It is everything which is made. I was amazed that it could last, for I thought that it was so little that it could suddenly fall into nothing. And I was answered in my understanding: It lasts and always will, because God loves it; and thus everything has being through the love of God.[28]

The late twentieth century is a skeptical time, with God's Nietzschean death noted long ago. But the modern woman makes clear her view that Julian's vision is not simply the product of a fuzzy-headed ascetic whose insight is the result of a peculiar dementia or the absence of experience. The vision speaks to Levertov precisely because she imagines the anchoress Julian having not only lived an enclosed life, but having been a woman in the world. These are visions of desire, not denial.

Interpreting and imagining a life for Julian, of whom little is known, Levertov observes that "What she petitioned for was never / instead of something else." She craved and received the full range of human experience. Though "She had not married," she "was no starveling" for intense emotion: "if she had loved, / she had been loved." And though "Death or some other destiny / bore him away, death or some other bride / changed him" (*Breathing* 76) this audacious "vivid woman" (77), embracing the necessity of change, found more than solace in a new life of study and spirit:

> Somehow,
> reading or read to, she'd spiralled
> up within tall towers
> of learning, steeples of discourse.
> Bells in her spirit
> rang new changes. (76)

The strength of the vision lies in the strength of the woman, discovered in her prose by Levertov, and in Levertov's verse by a reader likely to be unfamiliar with Julian's own writings.

To understand Julian, the poet proclaims, one must broadly imagine her world and the probable particulars of her routine experience as well as the details of her miraculous moment. Creating a biography for her, Levertov envisions an intensely demanding physical environment where the artfully crafted formal structures of religion were a vivid presence amidst man's intimate connection with the natural world. She offers glimpses of a beginning, a childhood place: "the dairy's bowls of clabber, of rich cream, / ghost-white in shade." Here we can imagine the sensory intensity of Julian's activity as she "run[s] back and forth, into the chill again, / the sweat of slate . . . / . . . / hot light, hot / wood, the swinging gate," in the shadow of the ever present "spire" which "split the blue / between two trees, a half-century old—/ she thought it ancient." The busy, flowing, and changeable physical rural life seems to intermingle with the formal solidity and wonder of the spiritual, each enriching the other with its energies and substance: "Her father's hall, her mother's bower, / nothing was dull. The cuckoo / was changing its tune":

> In the church
> there was glass in the windows, glass
> colored like the world. You could see
> Christ and his mother and his cross,
> you could see his blood, and the throne of God.
> In the fields
> calves were lowing, the shepherd was taking the sheep
> to new pasture.
>
> *(Breathing* 77)

Demystifying Julian, enabling the reader to envision her in youth and to feel her vitality and wonder, Levertov offers clues that allow comprehension of Julian's adult commitment to contact with a supreme love.

As the physical and spiritual were mixed in her sight daily as she grew, so they are in the intensities of her seeking after religious revelation. "To desire wounds" (*Breathing* 76), what Julian calls in *Showings* "the wound of contrition, the wound of compassion and the wound of longing with my will for God,"[29] is "not, five centuries early, neurosis," Levertov insists. It is rather the urge to understand by merging physical and spiritual into each other:

> . . . the desire to enact metaphor, for flesh to make known
> to intellect (as uttered song
>   makes known to voice,
>   as image to eye)
> make known in bone and breath
> (and not die) God's agony. (76)

Spiritual revelation illuminates and is clarified by lived experience. "God's wounded hand" reaching out to place in Julian's "the entire world" is understood in the memory of "one day / of infant light" when "her mother might have given / into her two cupped palms / a newlaid egg, warm from the hen," or when in the same way her brother "risked to her solemn joy / his delicate treasure / a sparrow's egg from the hedgerow." To recognize the connection of vision with memory stored in the individual consciousness, Levertov suggests, is not to diminish revelation, but to enrich it with human understanding. If people know themselves they may come to perceive God's presence in the world, and recognizing His kinship with them they find that:

> God for a moment in our history
> placed in that five-fingered
> human nest
> the macrocosmic egg, sublime paradox,
> brown hazelnut of All that Is—
> made, and belov'd, and preserved.
> As still, waking each day within
> our microcosm, we find it, and ourselves.
>
> (*Breathing* 78)

Committed here, as throughout her full career, to the truths of the physical world, yet without skepticism regarding spiritual belief, Levertov finds in Julian a resonance of experience that speaks to her own modern moment. Knowing that Julian's recognitions are open "to dismissive judgements / flung backward down the centuries—/ 'delirium,' 'hallucination,' " she asserts, nonetheless, the significance of that life:

> She lived in dark times, as we do:
> war, and the Black Death, hunger, strife,
> torture, massacre. She knew
> All of this, she felt it.
>
> (*Breathing* 81)

In her ability to know confusion and suffering yet to take joy in experience, laughing "In scorn of malice" (*Breathing* 79) and buoyed by her close contact with both the worlds of things and of spirit, and by her fierce certainty of pervasive love, Julian offers up the truths of her commitment. "Julian, Julian—/ I turn to you,"

Levertov writes, for "you clung to joy though tears and sweat / rolled down your face":

> clung like an acrobat, by your teeth fiercely,
> to a cobweb-thin high-wire, your certainty
> of infinite mercy, witnessed
> with your own eyes, with outward sight
> in your small room, with inward sight
> in your untrammeled spirit—
> knowledge we long to share:
> *Love was his meaning.* (82)

Whether Levertov is using her own "outward sight," observing with minute particular attention the "ancient / stones" of "La Cordelle" (*Breathing* 73), a small chapel below Vézelay, or offering her "inward sight" in a wrenching meditation of grief "During a Son's Dangerous Illness" (34), the poems of *Breathing the Water* are illuminated by a similar "untrammeled spirit." Forty-seven years after her first published poem, she continues to discover ways of fulfilling her own stated goals for fine writing. *Breathing the Water* "sets in motion . . . elements in the reader that otherwise would be stagnant. And that movement . . . cannot be without importance if one conceives of the human being as one in which all the parts are so related that none completely fulfills its function unless all are active" (*Poet* 6).

DECIPHERING THE SPIRIT

Notes

1. Joan F. Hallisey, "Invocations of Humanity: Denise Levertov's Poetry of Emotion and Belief," *Sojourners: An Independent Christian Monthly* (Feb. 1986): 34, 36.

2. Nathan A. Scott, Jr., *The Poetics of Belief* (Chapel Hill: University of North Carolina Press, 1985) 6.

3. Philip Wheelwright, *The Burning Fountain: A Study in the Language of Symbolism*, new and rev. ed. (Bloomington: Indiana University Press, 1968) 18.

4. The discussion here incorporates a portion of my "Denise Levertov, *Life in the Forest*," *New England Review*, 2 (1979): 162–64.

5. Cesare Pavese, *Hard Labor*, trans. William Arrowsmith (New York: Grossman, 1976) 100–01.

6. For examples of Pavese's extremely direct descriptions of people and places, see "A Season" (*Hard Labor* 65) and "Simplicity": "In the winter fog / the man lives jailed between streets, drinking / his cold water, biting his crust of bread" (91).

7. This draws from my article "Exploring the Human Community: The Poetry of Denise Levertov and Muriel Rukeyser," *Sagetrieb*, 3 (Winter 1984).

8. Denise Levertov, "A Poet's View," *Religion and Intellectual Life* 1 (Summer 1984): 48.

9. Levertov, "A Poet's View" 52–53.

10. William Carlos Williams, *Paterson* (New York: New Directions, 1963) 6. The phrase appears in many places in Williams's writing.

11. Denise Levertov, "The Ideas in the Things," in *Ezra Pound and William Carlos Williams: The University of Pennsylvania Conference Papers*, ed. Daniel Hoffman (Philadelphia: University of Pennsylvania Press, 1983) 131.

12. See John 14:2. The KJV uses the word "mansions"; in the RSV it is "rooms."

13. Denise Levertov, "Gathered at the River: Background and Form," typescript of an unpublished article 4.

14. Hallisey, "Invocations" 36.

15. Stanley Kunitz, *A Kind of Order, A Kind of Folly* (Boston: Little, Brown, 1975) 54.

16. Samuel Taylor Coleridge, "This Lime-Tree Bower My Prison," *Coleridge Poetical Works*, ed. Ernest Hartley Coleridge (London: Oxford University Press, 1969) 179, 181. This edition, initially published by Oxford University Press in 1912 in the Oxford Standard Authors Series under the title *The Poems of Samuel Taylor Coleridge*, was first reprinted with its present title in 1967.

17. Hallisey, "Invocations" 35.

18. Denise Levertov, " . . . That Passeth All Understanding," *Oblique Prayers* 85. For the sake of concision this title will be shortened hereafter to "Understanding" in citations that appear parenthetically in the text.

19. See "Notes" to *Breathing the Water*, p. 85, for a summary of Levertov's sources for her two groups of what she calls "Spinoffs."

20. J. B. Leishman, trans. Rainer Maria Rilke, *Selected Works, Volume II: Poetry* (New York: New Directions, 1960) 27.

21. Rilke, *Selected Works* 28.

22. Rilke, *Selected Works* 29.

23. See H. W. Janson, *History of Art* (Englewood Cliffs, NJ: Prentice-Hall and New York: Harry N. Abrams, Inc., 1962) 269, 289–90, 428, 513, for useful commentary on depictions of Christ by the artists Levertov mentions in this poem. For visual examples, see in Janson the reproductions of Giotto: "Christ Entering Jerusalem" (1305–06) 238; Van Eyck: "The Crucifixion," "The Last Judgment" (*c.* 1420–25) 275; Rembrandt: "Christ Preaching," (*c.* 1652) 428; Rouault: "Head of Christ," (1905) 513.

24. Rilke, *Selected Works* 30.

25. See Luke 24:13–35.

26. In a note of Sept. 15, 1987, Levertov wrote to the author pointing out a misprint on p. 66 of *Breathing the Water*. Line 16 should read "But she in the kitchen" rather than "But she is in the kitchen" as it is currently printed.

27. See the "Introduction," to Julian of Norwich, *Showings*, trans., introd. Edmund Colledge, O.S.A., and James Walsh, S.J., pref. Jean Leclercq (New York: Paulist, 1978) 18.

DECIPHERING THE SPIRIT

28. Julian of Norwich, *Showings* 130. This passage is from the "Short Text" of Julian's work.

29. Julian of Norwich, *Showings* 127.

BIBLIOGRAPHY

Works by Denise Levertov

The list of Denise Levertov's publications includes books from trade publishers. It does not include the many limited editions of her poems that have been published.

Books

The Double Image. London: Cresset, 1946. *P - P.*

Here and Now. San Francisco: City Lights Books, 1957.

Overland to the Islands. Highlands, NC: Jargon, 1958.

With Eyes at the Back of Our Heads. New York: New Directions, 1959.

The Jacob's Ladder. New York: New Directions, 1961; London: Cape, 1965.

O Taste and See. New York: New Directions, 1964.

The Sorrow Dance. New York: New Directions, 1967; London: Cape, 1968.

Selected Poems of Guillevic (Translations). New York: New Directions, 1969.

Relearning the Alphabet. New York: New Directions, 1970; London: Cape, 1970.

To Stay Alive. New York: New Directions, 1971.

Footprints. New York: New Directions, 1972.

The Poet in the World (Prose). New York: New Directions, 1973.

The Freeing of the Dust. New York: New Directions, 1975.

Life in the Forest. New York: New Directions, 1978.

Collected Earlier Poems 1940–1960. New York: New Directions, 1979.

Light Up the Cave (Prose). New York: New Directions, 1981.

BIBLIOGRAPHY

Candles in Babylon. New York: New Directions, 1982.
Poems 1960–1967. New York: New Directions, 1983.
Oblique Prayers. New York: New Directions, 1984; Newcastle-upon-Tyne: Bloodaxe, 1986.
Selected Poems. Newcastle-upon-Tyne: Bloodaxe, 1986.
Poems 1968–1972. New York: New Directions, 1987.
Breathing the Water. New York: New Directions, 1987.

Selected Uncollected Prose

"Denise Levertov." Contributor's note in *The New American Poetry: 1945–1960*. Ed. Donald M. Allen. New York: Grove, London: Evergreen, 1960 440–41.

"Foreword." In *Where Silence Reigns: Selected Prose by Rainer Maria Rilke*. Trans. G. Craig Houston. New York: New Directions, 1978 iv–vi.

"The Ideas in the Things." In *Ezra Pound and William Carlos Williams: The University of Pennsylvania Conference Papers*. Ed. Daniel Hoffman. Philadelphia: University of Pennsylvania Press, 1983 131–42.

"Remembering Kenneth Rexroth." *American Poetry Review* 12 (Jan.–Feb. 1983): 18–19.

"A Poet's View." *Religion and Intellectual Life* 1 (Summer 1984): 46–53.

"On Williams' Triadic Line; or How to Dance on Variable Feet." *Ironwood* 12 (Fall 1984): 95–102.

"Denise Levertov Writes." In *The Bloodaxe Book of Contemporary Women Poets: Eleven British Writers*. Ed. Jeni Couzyn. Newcastle-upon-Tyne: Bloodaxe, 1985 75–79.

Interviews

Atchity, Kenneth John. "An Interview with Denise Levertov." *San Francisco Review of Books* (March 1979): 5–8.

BIBLIOGRAPHY

Hallisey, Joan F. "Invocations of Humanity: Denise Levertov's Poetry of Emotion and Belief." *Sojourners: An Independent Christian Monthly* (Feb. 1986): 32–36.

Packard, William. "Craft Interview with Denise Levertov." *The New York Quarterly* 7 (Summer 1971): 9–25. Reprinted in *The Craft of Poetry: Interviews from The New York Quarterly*. Ed. William Packard. Garden City, NY: Doubleday, 1974; and *The Poet's Craft: Interviews from the New York Quarterly*. Ed. William Packard. New York: Paragon House, 1987.

Reid, Ian. " 'Everyman's Land': Ian Reid Interviews Denise Levertov." *Southern Review* (Adelaide, Australia) 5 (1972): 231–36.

Smith, Lorrie. "An Interview with Denise Levertov." *Michigan Quarterly Review* 24 (1985): 596–604.

Sutton, Walter. "Conversation with Denise Levertov." *The Minnesota Review* 5 (1965): 322–38.

Zwicky, Fay. "An Interview with Denise Levertov." *Westerly* 2 (July 1979): 119–26.

Books About Denise Levertov

Wagner, Linda Welshimer. *Denise Levertov*. New York: Twayne, 1967. A useful overview, organized topically, of Levertov's work through *O Taste and See*. Offers a brief chronology and a selected bibliography of primary and secondary sources.

——— ed., introd. *Denise Levertov: In Her Own Province*. New York: New Directions, 1979. Reprints interviews with Levertov, essays by her, essays and reviews about her work by Robert Pack, Albert Gelpi, and others. Levertov has pointed out misprints, misspellings, and other editorial errors which suggest that readers should consult original sources.

BIBLIOGRAPHY

Selected Parts of Books

Altieri, Charles. *Enlarging the Temple: New Directions in Poetry during the 1960's*. Lewisburg: Bucknell University Press, 1980; London: Associated University Presses, 1980. The chapter on "Denise Levertov and the Limits of the Aesthetics of Presence" explains the "inadequacy" of Levertov's "objectivist" aesthetic of "presence as plenitude" when she tries to adapt to "pressing social concerns caused by the war in Vietnam" (226).

Carruth, Hayden. *Working Papers: Selected Essays and Reviews*. Ed. Judith Weissman. Athens: University of Georgia Press, 1982. "Two Books," a review of *Overland to the Islands* and Lawrence Ferlinghetti's *A Coney Island of the Mind*, suggests that Levertov is "much closer to the French than to the San Francisco school" (27). Review-essay of *The Poet in the World*, collected here as "Levertov," discusses among other subjects her neoplatonism, her musical language, and her notion from Gerard Manley Hopkins of inscape.

Howard, Richard. *Alone With America: Essays on the Art of Poetry in the United States Since 1950*. Enl. ed. New York: Atheneum, 1980. Levertov entry discusses the development of her idiosyncratic voice, the autobiographical elements of her writing, and her response to the American language. Levertov is seen to combine the domestic and the dutiful with the sacramental.

Juhasz, Suzanne. *Naked and Fiery Forms: Modern American Poetry by Women, A New Tradition*. New York: Octagon, 1976. The chapter entitled " 'The Enactment of Rites': The Poetry of Denise Levertov" concludes that Levertov's work derives from a "masculine tradition that dominates modern poetry," but that her poetry also contains elements of an "emerging feminine" tradition (58).

BIBLIOGRAPHY

Lacey, Paul A. *The Inner War: Forms and Themes in Recent American Poetry*. Philadelphia: Fortress, 1972. The chapter "A Poetry of Exploration" presents a thoughtful overview of Levertov's "language of mystery" (110), examining, among other subjects, her developing vision of evil and the role of art in a troubled time.

Malkoff, Karl. *Crowell's Handbook of Contemporary American Poetry*. New York: Crowell, 1973. Useful for its extensive introductory survey of poetry since the Second World War. Specific entry on Levertov discusses her sympathy with "the mystic's way of knowing" (175) as well as her interest in ordinary experience.

Mersmann, James F. *Out of the Vietnam Vortex*. Lawrence: University Press of Kansas, 1974. The chapter entitled "Denise Levertov: Piercing In" presents a clear overview of Levertov's work through *To Stay Alive*. Close readings of *The Sorrow Dance* and *Relearning the Alphabet* in particular suggest ways Levertov reacts to war as "a violation of the innate order at the heart of things" (79).

Mills, Ralph J., Jr. *Contemporary American Poetry*. New York: Random House, 1965. The chapter entitled "Denise Levertov" offers an important appreciation. Examines Levertov's early interest in Surrealism, her relation to Rilke, Pound, Williams, Eliot, Creeley, others, and her themes and techniques.

———. *Cry of the Human: Essays on Contemporary American Poetry*. Urbana: University of Illinois Press, 1975. A perceptive chapter, "Creation's Very Self: On the Personal Element in Recent American Poetry," discusses Levertov's poems in relation to the issue of the centrality of the self in contemporary poetry.

Rexroth, Kenneth. *American Poetry in the Twentieth Century*. New York: Herder, 1971. As part of a lively critical survey of

BIBLIOGRAPHY

poetry in England and America during and after the Second World War, Rexroth places Levertov amidst her contemporaries and discusses her special relationship to women poets of the century.

———. *Assays*. New York: New Directions, 1961. Wide ranging and influential review of *Here and Now*, collected here as "Denise Levertov" in the section "Poets Old and New," concludes that Levertov is "incomparably the best poet of what is getting to be known as the new avant-garde" (231).

——— ed., introd. *The New British Poets: An Anthology*. New York: New Directions, 1949. Informative "Introduction" locates Levertov amidst the "New Romanticism" (xiv) of British poetry in the years during and immediately following the Second World War.

Rosenthal, M. L. *The New Poets: American and British Poetry Since World War II*. London: Oxford University Press, 1967. Brief though pointed discussion of Levertov's development through *O Taste and See* viewed in light of the work of Black Mountain writers.

Stepanchev, Stephen. *American Poetry since 1945*. New York: Harper and Row, 1965. Surveys Levertov's work from *The Double Image* through *O Taste and See*. Discusses Levertov's relationship to Olson, Duncan, and Creeley, praising her growing powers of exact observation.

Thurley, Geoffrey. *The American Moment: American Poetry in the Mid-Century*. London: Edward Arnold, 1972. Concludes in the chapter "Phenomenalist Idioms: Doolittle, Moore, Levertov" that Levertov is one of a generation of post-Second World War phenomenalist poets whose living space coincides with their aesthetic space.

Selected Articles

Aiken, William. "Denise Levertov, Robert Duncan, and Allen

BIBLIOGRAPHY

Ginsberg: Modes of Self in Projective Poetry." *Modern Poetry Studies* 10 (1981): 200–40. Analysis of Levertov and Duncan as representing differing tendencies in organic poetry—Levertov the outward, visual, and phenomenal, Duncan the inward, aural, and personal. Sees their tendencies combining in the work of Ginsberg.

Bowering, George. "Denise Levertov." *The Antigonish Review* 7 (Autumn 1971): 76–87. Overview of Levertov as a poet "looking for a way to be the complete woman and poet" (87) in a fragmented world. Uses Anne Bradstreet and Emily Dickinson as touchstones.

Carruth, Hayden. "What 'Organic' Means?" *Sagetrieb* 4 (Spring 1985): 145–46. A speculation upon the nature of Levertov's subjectivity that mixes observation, meditation, and memory.

Costello, Bonnie. "Flooded with Otherness." *Parnassus* 8 (Fall–Winter 1979): 198–212. A review-essay on *Freeing the Dust, Life in the Forest, Collected Earlier Poems 1940–1960*. Concludes generally that in searching for equilibrium Levertov's verse has become posed and inauthentic. Finds that Levertov distorts reality, though in some of the late poems of *Life in the Forest* her mature voice can be heard once again.

Duddy, Thomas A. "To Celebrate: A Reading of Denise Levertov." *Criticism* 10 (Spring 1968): 138–52. Discusses Levertov as a poet who, through the imagination, celebrates the present moment. Links Levertov to the English Romantics, especially to Keats, Wordsworth, and Blake.

DuPlessis, Rachel Blau. "The Critique of Consciousness and Myth in Levertov, Rich and Rukeyser." *Feminist Studies* 3 (Fall 1975): 199–221. Reprinted in *Shakespeare's Sisters*. Eds. Sandra M. Gilbert and Susan Gubar. Bloomington: Indiana University Press, 1979. Provocative article which discusses ways the three poets offer acts of criticism and statements of

BIBLIOGRAPHY

personal awakening to political and social life (199) in poems about women, war and politics, and myth.

Gilbert, Sandra M. "Revolutionary Love: Denise Levertov and the Poetics of Politics." *Parnassus* 12–13 (Spring–Winter 1985): 335–51. A broad survey of Levertov's work which finds that her most revolutionary gesture is an articulation of joy in being. Observes that Levertov's poems about womanhood and relationships are most successful. By-and-large her directly political poems are insufficiently poetical. Prefers Bly, Lowell, and Shelley as political poets.

Gitzen, Julian. "From Reverence to Attention: The Poetry of Denise Levertov." *Midwest Quarterly* 16 (1975): 325–41. Surveys Levertov's work as poetry that "celebrates strenuous life" and "makes movement a virtue" (334).

Hallisey, Joan F. "Denise Levertov's 'Illustrious Ancestors': The Hassidic Influence." *Melus* 9 (Winter II 1982): 5–11. A useful biographical reading which focuses on Levertov's knowledge of, and connection to, Hasidic thought, lore, and tales.

Harris, Victoria. "The Incorporative Consciousness: Levertov's Journey from Discretion to Unity." *Exploration* 4 (Dec. 1976): 33–48. Thoughtful explications, primarily of *O Taste and See*. Defines the relationship to reality which informs Levertov's poetic voice, suggesting that Levertov's poetic consciousness balances "centripetal motion which brings in the sensory landscape" with "centrifugal forces issuing from the poet herself" (33).

Kyle, Carol A. "Every Step an Arrival: *Six Variations* and the Musical Structure of Denise Levertov's Poetry." *The Centennial Review* 17 (1973): 281–96. Suggestive formal analysis of the general musical structure of Levertov's poetry, concentrating on "Six Variations" but discussing the range of Levertov's work through *Footprints*.

BIBLIOGRAPHY

Lacey, Paul A. "The Poetry of Political Anguish." *Sagetrieb* 4 (Spring 1985): 61–71. Careful reading of *To Stay Alive* to suggest how political themes, language, and commitments are expressed in Levertov's poetry which is, at its best, didactic and lyrical.

Marten, Harry. "Exploring the Human Community: The Poetry of Denise Levertov and Muriel Rukeyser." *Sagetrieb* 3 (Winter 1984): 51–61. The relationship of Levertov's poetry to Rukeyser's, two poets who seek in form and theme to reveal and define the relationship of the individual to his or her community.

Ostriker, Alicia. "In Mind: The Divided Self and Women's Poetry." *Midwest Quarterly* 24 (1983): 351–65. The wild self and the tame self in Levertov's work, viewed in relation to the divided self in the poems of Diane Wakoski, Sylvia Plath, Adrienne Rich, Margaret Atwood, Louise Glück, and others. Uses R. D. Laing on schizophrenia for a framework in psychology.

Smith, Lorrie. "Songs of Experience: Denise Levertov's Political Poetry." *Contemporary Literature* 27 (1986): 213–32. Illuminating analysis of the ways Levertov's ethical imagination has grappled for twenty years with the relationship of public life and politics to personal life and religious conviction. Explores Levertov's changing notions of how to present and deal with evil in the world.

Surman, Diana. "Inside and outside in the poetry of Denise Levertov." *Critical Quarterly* 22 (Spring 1980): 57–70. Levertov thoughtfully placed amidst Objectivists, Romantics, Black Mountaineers, Eliot, Williams, and others. Critical overview of the interrelationship between self and objects in Levertov's work.

Wagner, Linda. "Levertov and Rich: The Later Poems." *The*

BIBLIOGRAPHY

South Carolina Review 11 (Spring 1979): 18–27. Suggests that Levertov in *Footprints* and *The Freeing of the Dust* and Rich in *The Will to Change, Diving into the Wreck,* and *Poems, Selected and New* explore the full range of the psyche, writing "a poetry that speaks for life in the late 1970's" (27). Levertov still expresses her early convictions of the poet's responsibilities, but the bitterness of some of her earlier social writing has mellowed toward tranquility.

Younkins, Ronald. "Denise Levertov and the Hasidic Tradition." *Descant* 19 (Fall 1974): 40–48. Informative explanation of Levertov's use of Hasidic tales and philosophies in her poems of the 1960s.

INDEX

INDEX